Late Night with David Letterman: The Book

~~THE DAY THE WHISTLING STOPPED: THE SHORT, TRAGIC LIFE OF HARRIET ZWINDEL~~

Late Night with David Letterman: The Book

Edited by

Merrill Markoe

Written by

Andy Breckman	Tom Gammil	George Meyer
Randy Cohen	Fred Graver	Gerard Mulligan
Kevin Curran	Larry Jacobson	Steve O'Donnell
Jim Downey	David Letterman	Max Pross
Chris Elliott	Merrill Markoe	Joe Toplyn
Sanford Frank	Jeff Martin	Matt Wickline

Villard Books New York 1985

Library of Congress Cataloging in Publication Data
Letterman, David.
    Late night with David Letterman: the book.
    I. Markoe, Merrill.   II. Title.
PN1992.77.L38L48   1985   791.45'72   85-40390
ISBN 0-394-74191-9

The photographs used as chapter headings in this
book were all conceived, designed and produced
by Marc Karzen (photographer), Bob Pook (graphic
art director), and Edd Hall (visuals coordinator).
In television, these images are referred to as
"bumpers" and can be seen before and after commercials on _Late Night_.

Manufactured in the United States of America

9 8 7 6 5 4 3 2

First Edition

Text Design by Marsha Cohen/Parallelogram

To the staff and crew of *Late Night*,
and all their parents, who worked so hard making
the costumes

Acknowledgments

Scenic Designers

Kathleen Ankers
Jeremy Conway

Scenic Artists

Joseph Konopka
Margot Therre
Carole Lee Carroll

Art Researcher

Edd Hall

Photographer

Marc Karzen

Outside Props

Dan Bleier

Graphic Artists

Bob Pook
William Shortridge, Jr.
Arlen Schumer
Dennis Francis
Anne Healy
Roger White

Also, the rest of our staff, in alphabetical order:

Lis Anderson
Eric Anthony
Glenn Arber
Peter Basil
Nina Beber
Jude Brennan
Hiram Bullock
Candy Carrell
Calvert DeForest
Laurie Diamond
Jack Dolan
Carl Eckett
Mandy Fatovich
Pete Fatovich
Al Frisch
Sandra Furton
Barbara Gaines
Eddie Gorodetsky

Elmer Govey
Hal Gurnee
Laurie Guthrie
Liza Hall
Sue Hall
Darcy Hettrich
Susan Hum
Paul Johnston
Steve Jordan
Bill Kenny
Will Lee
Laurie Lennard
George Magda
Gene Martin
Brian McAloon
Sid McGinnis
Gae Morris
Robert Morton

Paula Niedert
Marie O'Donnell
Pat O'Keefe
Jay Ottley
Maria Pope
Jack Rollins
Bob Rudick
Barry Sand
Jaymie Sayet
Rick Scheckman
Paul Shaffer
Barbara Sheehan
Betsey Steyer
Cheryl Thacker
Karl Tiedeman
Cathy Vasapoli
Howard Vinitsky
Steve Weiner

Contents

Intro by Dave

Dear Reader,

Congratulations on your fine purchase and get set to experience what we believe to be the ultimate test of man and machine. Oh! No, I'm sorry. That's the Indianapolis 500. Which, by the way, smells like burning rubber. Believe me, it would be quite a mess for your coffeetable, bookshelf, or loved one. You're very lucky this is just a book. Although it's really hard to think of it as *just* a book, now isn't it?

When we were first approached by the President's Council on Medium-Priced Trade Paperback Publications, frankly we were skeptical. But as the project unfolded, those feelings were quickly replaced by uncertainty. We want you to think of this book not merely as a book, but as a book that would have contained many more color photographs had the price been jerked up a couple of dollars.

You know, some have called me moody, bitter, brooding, even hypoglycemic. But it is my fervent hope to let you, Dear Reader, judge for yourself. I do know one thing for sure: never before in modern history has the love of a man for a woman burned more brightly than between the covers of this explicit bombshell. Which, personally, I'll take any day over more color photographs.

I certainly hope you've enjoyed these few minutes together. In writing this intro, it was my hope to welcome you all to our book, make you feel at home and, yes, to perhaps even take your beverage order. But in rereading my efforts now, I see that what I've really been able to do is minimize the number of blank pages at the front. We think you'll agree.

Thank you. Good night. Drive safely.
Your friend,

David Letterman

Editor's Foreword

by Merrill Markoe

One of the real benefits of a continued association with *Late Night* has always been an unlimited opportunity to spend time with dogs. This has proven to be time that has enriched my life immeasurably as I slowly found myself beginning to spiritually profit from the simple yet profound way in which they order their lives. And now that I have finally begun to apply the things I have learned, I see that at last my life has begun to make sense. That is why I want to share with you, in this important forum, these rules for living that have brought new peace and sanity to my world.

What the Dogs Have Taught Me

Daily Routine

The day is divided into two important sections.
Mealtime. And *everything else*.

I. Mealtime

1. Just because there does not seem to be anything *visible* around to eat certainly does not mean there is *nothing* around to eat. The act of staring at the underside of a table or chair on which someone else is eating sets in motion a chain of events that eventually results in food.
2. It goes without saying that you should carefully check the lower third of *any* space for edibles. Mouth-sized things which cannot be identified by sight or smell are considered gum.

3. When you actually receive a meal, submerge your head into it as you would a shower. *Never, ever* look up again until a minimum of at least fifteen minutes after the obvious food is gone. This is important. Just because your dish is empty does not mean that it is time to stop eating.
4. Remember that *all* food is potentially yours up until the time that it is actually swallowed by another. The lengthy path a piece of food will take from a plate to a mouth via a hand is as good a time as any to stake your claim to it.
5. When it comes to selecting an appropriate beverage, location and packaging mean *nothing*. There are *absolutely no exceptions* to this rule.
6. If you really see something you want, and all your other attempts at getting it have failed, it is only right to grovel shamelessly. As a second tactic, stare intently at the object of your desire, allowing long gelatinous drools to leak like icicles from your lower lip.

II. Everything Else

1. There are really only two important facial expressions to bother with: *complete overwhelming joy* and *nothing at all*.
2. Any time that is not meal time is potentially nap time. The best time to take a nap is when you hear your name being called repeatedly. The best location for a nap is dead center of any street or driveway. The most relaxing position is on your side, all four limbs parallel.
3. The most practical way to get dry is to shake violently near a fully clothed person. A second effective method is to stand on a light-colored piece of furniture.
4. *Personal Security*
   A. At the first hint of any irregular noise, run from room to room yelling loudly. If someone actually comes into the house, rush over to them whether you know them or not. Then kiss them so violently that they lose their balance or have to force you away physically.
   B. The greatest unacknowledged threat to life as we have come to know it is squirrels. No matter what you must do, make sure there are none in your yard.
5. *Recreation and Leisure*
   A. *Ball:* There are two equally amusing sets of rules you will want to know.
      a. *The common form*, in which you receive a thrown ball and return it.
      b. *The preferred form*, in which you receive a thrown ball and eat it.
   B. *Car:* As you know, any open car door is an invitation to get in. Once inside, your only goal is to try to get out.
6. *Health*
   A. In the event of a trip to the doctor, always be on your guard. If you are vaccinated, urinate on the physician.

Afterword to Editor's Foreword

Since I have taken to sleeping under the bed, I have come to know tranquillity I never imagined possible.

   You never really know when it might be cookie time. And that's what the dogs have taught me.

Opening Remarks

An ancient Chinese proverb tells us that "The journey of a thousand miles begins with but a single step." And so too does fifty-seven minutes of late-night network television time begin with one lame joke.

What follows is a selection of our "opening remarks" that have won major international awards or been the basis of critically acclaimed TV movies or both.

The world was saddened by the recent passing of Dr. John Rock, who, of course, was famous for helping to develop the birth control pill. He was survived by his wife and what probably would have been four children.

Interesting survey in the current *Journal of Abnormal Psychology:* New York City has a higher percentage of people you shouldn't make any sudden moves around than any other city in the world.

Tourists—have some fun with New York's hard-boiled cabbies. When you get to your destination, say to your driver, "Pay? I was hitchhiking."

The space shuttle *Challenger* reported today that the only two human structures on earth visible from deep space are the Great Wall of China and Tip O'Neill.

Tip to out-of-town visitors: If you buy something here in New York and want to have it shipped home, be suspicious if the clerk tells you they don't need your name and address.

New Connecticut license-plate slogan: The Middle "C" Is Silent.

As most people know, Menudo has a policy of getting rid of members once they turn sixteen. What I *didn't* know is that the Grateful Dead have a similar policy, except their cutoff age is sixty.

There was an interesting development at the CBS-Westmoreland trial: both sides agreed that after the trial, Andy Rooney would be allowed to talk to the jury for three minutes about little things that annoyed him during the trial.

According to the new *Rand-McNally Places-Rated Almanac,* the best place to live in America is the city of Pittsburgh. The city of New York came in twenty-fifth. Here in New York we really don't care too much. Because we know that we could beat up their city anytime.

Today at lunchtime in midtown, a group of stunned New Yorkers stood on the sidewalk with their mouths open, pointing at something that obviously paralyzed them with amazement. Finally a tourist from Boston came along and explained that it was a parking space.

I read an interview with a man who had been technically dead for ten minutes. Asked to describe that period, he said, "It was like listening to Phil Rizzuto during a rain delay."

In an interview with *U.S. News & World Report* this week, Secretary of State George Shultz was asked what he considers his proudest accomplishment. He said, "Winning the office pools on Andropov *and* Chernenko."

Martin Levine has passed away at the age of seventy-five. Mr. Levine had owned a movie-theater chain here in New York. The funeral will be on Thursday. At 2:15, 4:20, 6:30, 8:40, and 10:50.

The shuttle mission is winding down. The first civilian passenger, on the next shuttle flight, will be a schoolteacher. Eventually there will be commercial travel on the shuttle. It'll cost $10,000 to go to the moon . . . $9,000 if you leave from Newark.

It's been so hot in New York, Mickey Rooney has been dating Dolly Parton just for the shade—What the hell? . . . I'm sorry—somehow the copy for Bob Hope's summer special got mixed in with this. Sorry for any inconvenience it might have caused.

Interesting poll results reported in today's New York *Post:* people on the street in midtown Manhattan were asked whether they approved of the U.S. invasion of Grenada. Fifty-three percent said yes; 39 percent said no; and 8 percent said "Gimme a quarter?"

A man in New Jersey just won over $3 million in a lottery there. He chose his winning number by taking the first three digits of Raymond Burr's weight.

A new book by a former aide claims that Gerald Ford has an imaginary friend named Donny.

This warning from the FDA: Nothing you wear on your head during sex can help you avoid disease. So don't throw your money away on the so-called herpes hat.

This warning from the New York City Department of Health Fraud: Be suspicious of any doctor who tries to take your temperature with his finger.

Someone did a study on the three most-often-heard phrases in New York City. One is, "Hey, taxi." Two is, "What train do I take to get to Bloomingdale's?" And three is, "Don't worry. It's just a flesh wound."

Every year when it's Chinese New Year here in New York, there are fireworks going off at all hours. New York mothers calm their frightened children by telling them it's just gunfire.

James Ramseur, one of the shooting victims of Bernhard Goetz, apparently faked his own kidnapping. The police received a phone call that he had been kidnapped by two white men in a Cadillac. Later that night he was found sitting in his apartment building. He isn't that bright a guy. Apparently, they took him into the police station for questioning. Had him look through mug shots . . . and he picked out his own picture.

I was walking to work today, and this wino came up to me and said, "Give me five hundred dollars for a cup of coffee?" I said, "That's a lot of money for a cup of coffee." And he said, "Hey—I don't tell you how to do *your* job, you don't tell me how to do *mine.*"

On Nancy Reagan's recent birthday, she said she was fifty-nine, although records reportedly showed she was sixty-one. Her explanation: she doesn't count the two years she spent in the National Hockey League.

An anthropologist at Tulane has just come back from a field trip to New Guinea with reports of a tribe so primitive they have Tide but not new Tide with lemon-fresh Borax.

A professor at Johns Hopkins has come forth with an intriguing thought about a perennial question: he says that if an infinite number of monkeys sat typing at an infinite number of typewriters, the smell in the room would be unbearable.

New Jersey announced today that they were adopting a new license-plate slogan: New Jersey—Try Our Thick, Creamy Shakes.

Asked by reporters about his upcoming marriage to a forty-two-year-old woman, director Roman Polanski told reporters, "The way I look at it, she's the equivalent of three fourteen-year-olds."

I saw something in the paper the other day that's a good example of what they mean by federal waste: A professor of pharmacology at Penn State just got a grant of $150,000 from the U.S. Public Health Service to develop a time-release placebo.

The Museum of the Hard to Believe

Since the beginning of recorded history, man has been fascinated by the unusual and the bizarre. Who can explain our mysterious attraction to the outlandish and the peculiar? We are all strangely drawn to the unnatural and the weird. What *is* it about the fantastic and the unfamiliar that never fails to arouse the curiosity? The miraculous and the grotesque just seem to appeal to us. Unfortunately, items like these are hard to come by and difficult to verify. We had a much easier time putting together a list of half-baked jokes and amateurishly doctored photographs for a feature we call "The Museum of the Hard to Believe."

The Face That Looked Like a Rock

Here, for the first time, the strange case of Bill McClory—a Western tour guide who was so impressed by tourists' keen interest in natural rock formations that looked like human faces that, eager for fame, he had his own face surgically altered to resemble Alaska's Mt. McKinley. **Hard to believe!**

The Working Car Clock

This dashboard clock, which came with the car, a 1971 Pontiac, has worked for over fourteen years! **Hard to believe!**

The Man Who Fooled Merv Griffin!

Frank Beaute, in the studio audience of the popular talk show, told host Griffin that he was from Laramie, Wyoming, when he was in fact from the Laramie suburb of Taylor City! **Hard to believe!**

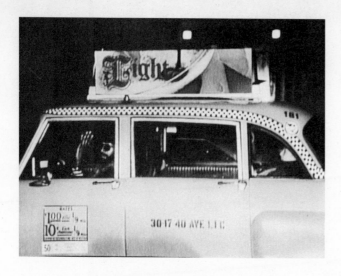

Cab

Now this one even I don't believe: ***The cab that stopped for a yellow light. Hard to believe!***

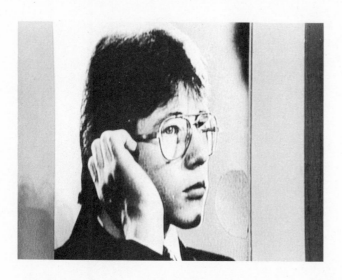

The Boy Who Kept His Word

This photo commemorates the famous **The boy who kept his word.** Jamie Larsen of Provo, Utah, asked a friend if he could "see his minibike for a second." Exactly one second later, he stopped looking at the minibike and went home. ***Hard to believe!***

Christie Hefner

This exhibit is entitled "The Incredible Coincidence." After Christie Hefner was named corporate head of Playboy Enterprises, it was discovered that the previous head of the same corporation was her father, Hugh Hefner. Statisticians say the odds against this occurring are five million to one. ***Hard to believe!***

The Truth About "Carpet"

Here's a surprising item entitled "Carpet: The Word That Lies Like a Rug" . . . the "carpet" is neither a "car" nor a "pet" . . . it *is*, however, a floor covering. **Hard to believe!**

The King Who Didn't Have Anything Really Odd or Eccentric About Him in Any Way

King Albert II of Moravia, 1640–1707, had no strange habits, always dressed properly, and never made any unreasonable demands or outlandish proclamations. He was finally overthrown and beheaded by bored peasants. **Hard to believe!**

The Paperweight That Tricked Destiny

By a bizarre twist of fate, a paperweight in Eugene, Oregon, was mistaken for an ashtray—and used for that purpose *for over twelve years!* **Hard to believe!!**

The Incredible Teen

Mike Calnosty, a sixteen-year-old boy who is not embarrassed to be seen with his parents. He actually asks them to school dances and doesn't mind if they drive him on dates. **Hard to believe!**

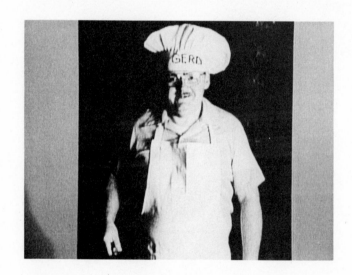

The Tight-Lipped Miracle Man

On a Monday, the last day of a long July Fourth weekend, holiday picnicker Gerd Topsnic was *not once* heard to utter, "Gee, doesn't today feel like a Sunday to you?" **Hard to believe!**

JUNE 7, 1983

PROGRAM CHART IS ON A-70

11:30 ❷ CBS MOVIE SPECIAL
1. Columbo.
An architect (Patrick O'Neal) murders a tycoon who refused to back his project. Columbo: Peter Falk.
2. Quincy.
A tycoon's death may be linked to —

The CBS Movie That Wasn't!

On Monday night, May 16, at 11:30, CBS presented *The CBS Movie Special*—but it was neither a movie *nor* was it special. It was an old *Columbo* episode followed by an old *Quincy* episode. **Hard to believe!**

The Incredible Mr. Marnek!

In 1978 Don Marnek went crazy and shot at passers-by from his apartment window with a high-powered rifle. Incredibly, when the police interviewed Marnek's neighbors, he was not described as a quiet man who kept to himself but as a "pushy loudmouth who stuck his nose in everyone's business." *Hard to believe!*

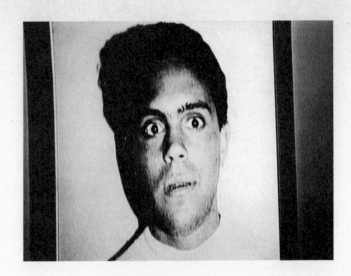

The Eyebrows of Mystery

Only a handful of network executives know television's best-kept secret. For the entire run of the hit series *Ironside,* actor Raymond Burr's original eyebrows were shaved off and replaced with a living pair of Arkansas ditch caterpillars. *Hard to believe!*

The Supreme Court: The Tenth Justice

The nine members of the Supreme Court have recently admitted an astonishing fact: for years now, they have never, never handed down a decision without first consulting the ghost of Elvis. *Hard to believe!*

The Demon Taxi

Yellow cab #534 has made the journey from Kennedy Airport to midtown Manhattan hundreds of times, and the meter usually totals around $20. But last week, when a Nigerian student boarded the cab on his first visit to America, the fare for his trip to midtown totaled a baffling $382. To this day that taxi's passenger cannot explain his astounding experience.

The Six-Pack of Mystery

This eerie carton of imported beers, purchased by L. D. Cutler of Webster Groves, Missouri, was later found to contain five Heinekens, and, strangely enough—a single bottle of Löwenbräu! *Hard to believe!*

The Man Without a Life-Style

Stud Selzman—the man without a life-style—lives with his parents and works for his father. "Maybe I have one but I don't know what it is," he says. *Hard to believe!*

The Bo Derek Board

This neatly sanded plank of cedarwood may not look familiar, but it's had a hand in several popular films recently. Yes, truly an unsung hero of Hollywood, this unassuming board has served as Bo Derek's acting coach since 1978. **Hard to believe!**

Godzilla's First Role

Trivia buffs will love this: a minor 1947 comedy called *Holiday in May* is now remembered for just one reason. It featured a walk-on by the then-unknown actor Buddy Zilla.... The young performer, who later of course changed his name to Godzilla, played a bit part as a traffic cop. Needless to say, he stole the scene. **Hard to believe!**

The Brain of Don Ameche

Repellent, yet oddly majestic—it's the brain of Don Ameche, preserved forever in this jar of formaldehyde. The most amazing thing about this exhibit is... Don Ameche is still alive! **Hard to believe!**

Black Elvis Man

Here's a startling exhibit—the black man in an Elvis movie! This crowd scene from *Viva Las Vegas*, magnified 600 times, clearly reveals a black actor in the background, obscured by some drapes. ***Hard to believe!***

The Statue of Liberty's Earrings

Here's an impressive piece of New York's history: the Statue of Liberty's earrings. They were left off at the last minute because they made her look "cheap." ***Hard to believe!***

ANDREW JACKSON
"OLD HICKORY"

The Eerie Paradox of Presidential Nicknames

Every school kid knows that Andrew Jackson was frequently called "Old Hickory," but do you recognize these other, less familiar presidential nicknames?

WILLIAM HOWARD TAFT
"THE FAT PIG"

JOHN QUINCY ADAMS
"OLD SCRATCH & SNIFF"

JAMES MONROE
"OLD BEANS 'N' FRANKS"

Ike's Heavy Chevy

Dwight Eisenhower won a second term in 1956 and earned a place in history when he rode to his second Inaugural in a souped-up, nitro-burning drag racer. The fuel-altered T-rail dragster—nicknamed "Ike's Heavy Chevy"—covered the distance from the reviewing stand to the Capitol steps in an incredible 6.2 seconds. It now tours with the Young Republicans Stunt Team and winters in the Eisenhower Library garage in Abilene. **Hard to believe!**

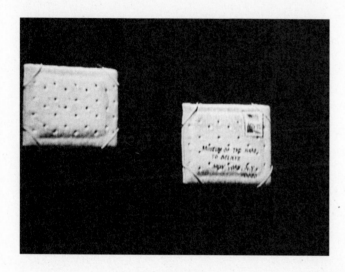

The Amazing Postable Pastry

A fascinating and true fact: the pop tart is the only food that can be mailed like a post card! And, incidentally, with no loss in flavor! **Hard to believe!**

David Letterman

They Took My Show Away
(An Afterschool Special)

Because our show comes on at such a late hour, we don't have the opportunity to reach as many pre-teens as we would like. So when NBC offered me the chance to star in an afterschool special aimed at the pre-teenage group, frankly, I was ecstatic. And I think you'll agree that even though it was made for kids, it deals with a subject that we all must face at one time or another.

"Jimmy, are you gonna do homework all night? Don't you think you should watch a little TV?"

"I will, Mr. Letterman. I just want to finish in time for my favorite show, *Voyagers*."

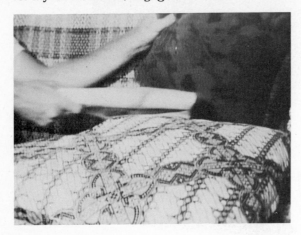

"Jimmy, what do you say we go for a little walk, all right?"

"You know what it means for a show to be canceled, Jimmy?"

"It's when a bunch of executives at a television network decide that a certain show shouldn't be on the air anymore. And then they take it off and replace it with something else."

"Sometimes it's a good idea because the show is filled with bad acting and bad writing."

"And sometimes it's the executives who have been bad."

"This canceled business. It could never happen to *Voyagers*, could it, Mr. Letterman?"
  "Yes, Jimmy. I'm afraid it has."

"Jimmy! Jimmy!"

"Jimmy! Jimmy!"

"Jimmy! I've been looking all over for you. Hold on there. Don't destroy that perfectly good *TV Guide*. Look—I know it hurts at first. But believe me, you're gonna get over it."

"You don't understand. Nobody does."

"Jimmy, just because a show is canceled doesn't mean it goes away forever. It can live on through reruns and syndication."

"You mean, I might see *Voyagers* again?"

"Well, maybe in some other form."

"You know, Jimmy, I remember when they canceled *The Six-Million-Dollar Man*. Boy! I thought my world was gonna end. But then *The Fall Guy* premiered and my prayers were answered."

"Sure, it was a different time and a slightly different format. But I adjusted, and you know what? I grew a little in the process."

"I know what you're saying, Mr. Letterman. But *Voyagers* was different. It was really special. I don't think I'll ever watch TV again."

"Jimmy . . . don't *ever* say that. Not even as a joke."

"Well, what should I do, Mr. Letterman?"

"Tell you what. I'll show you the new NBC fall schedule. I have a feeling we're gonna find a new show for you that may turn out to be as good as *Voyagers*."

"...and here's a show called *Manimal*. This one is about a crime fighter who can change into a snake and a bird."

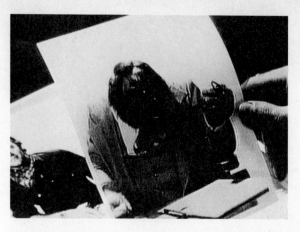

"This one is about a chimp who lives in Washington. You know that'll be good. Jimmy... I don't think we have anything to worry about."

"And to think I was sad because they canceled *Voyagers*. This is gonna be the best TV season ever."

"Maybe it will, Jimmy. Maybe it will."

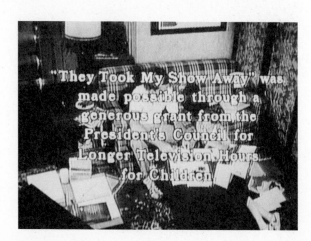

Frank and Fred

Frank and Fred at the Beach

One of America's favorite pastimes is going to the beach. But unless you know what you're doing, a day in the sun can turn into a hellish nightmare of social blunders, faux pas, and gaffes. So let's pay a visit to our old friends Frank and Fred as they demonstrate some "Beachgoing Do's and Don'ts."

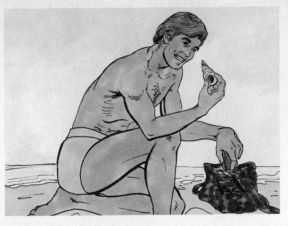

Fred enjoys exploring the beach and collecting unusual seashells.

Frank collects bikini tops.

Fred and his friends play Frisbee at a courteous distance from other beachgoers.

Frank and his friends practice their wheelies.

Fred is more than happy to rub baby oil on his date's back.

Frank smears his date's back with chopped fish.

Fred is forever awestruck by the beauty of the sea.

Frank blows his nose on his hand.

Fred changes the station on his radio to his date's favorite music.

Frank changes the oil in his car.

Fred plays it safe and wears a protective sunscreen.

Frank wears evil clown makeup.

Fred cautiously advises: No swimming for an hour after eating.

Frank says no eating for an hour after watching fat people play volleyball.

Spending the Night at Your Girlfriend's

Fred makes sure to look his best.

Frank also dresses carefully.

Fred brings his date a long-stemmed rose.

Frank brings a moist shoe tree.

Fred compliments his date on her apartment. He says, "I have that poster, too. It changed my life."

Frank picks up her turntable and says, "Hey, can I have this?"

After a big spaghetti dinner, Fred says, "What a great meal. It really sticks to the ribs."

Frank says, "What a great meal. It really sticks to the ceiling."

After dinner Fred lights a romantic fire.

Frank also lights a romantic fire.

Fred says, "Here. I'd like you to wear this."

Frank says, "Here. I'd like you to wear this."

Fred's date laughingly plays hard to get.

Frank's date also plays hard to get.

In bed, Fred is gentle and considerate of his partner's needs.

Frank keeps his Walkman on the whole time.

Afterward, Fred hugs his partner and whispers, "I love you."

Frank yells, "I won! I won!"

When Fred's date wakes up, she finds a marriage proposal and a wedding ring on the bureau.

When Frank's date wakes up, she finds an empty tube of Nair and her eyebrows missing.

How to Be a Good Houseguest

Fred wakes up to the sound of chirping birds.

Frank wakes up naked on the patio.

Fred helps Junior conduct scientific experiments.

So does Frank.

Fred plays with the kids in the den.

Frank plays with the kids on the roof.

Fred makes popcorn while the family watches home movies.

Frank makes loud noises with his body whenever Grandma comes on the screen.

Fred laughs politely at his host's anecdotes.

Frank laughs at his host's toupee.

"I'm going to make a little trip into town. Does anyone need anything?" Fred asks thoughtfully.

"I gotta see a guy about some stuff," Frank mumbles. "Don't wait up for me."

Fred copies down a list of family safety rules.

Frank copies down a list of family credit-card numbers.

When spending time at the home of a friend, Fred makes a point of remembering everyone's name.

Frank calls everyone "dude."

When asked to say grace before dinner, Fred offers a touching verse from Robert Frost.

When asked to say grace before dinner, Frank plays air guitar and mumbles the lyrics to "Radar Love."

Do's and Don'ts . . . on the Job

Fred has accepted a job with Barnett Industries because it offered him a challenging position with plenty of room for advancement.

Frank has accepted a job with Barnett Industries because it's next to Blimpies.

Fred tries to make his new office as comfortable as possible. He brings in a picture of his wife.

Likewise, Frank wants to make his office as comfortable as possible, and also brings in a picture of Fred's wife.

Fred gets a bonus after just four months in the company.

Frank gets a bonus after just four minutes in the company locker room.

During the weekly meetings, Fred is always thoughtful and attentive.

Frank suddenly interrupts the meeting with his impression of Deney Terio and Motion.

Fred only takes a day off if it's really important —like if he has to bury his grandmother.

Frank doesn't take the day off to bury his grandmother.

After one year Fred gets a big promotion because his boss loves hard work and dedication.

Frank gets a big promotion because his boss loves a stockboy named Raoul.

Fred doesn't expect his secretary to bring him coffee just because she's a woman.

Frank doesn't expect his secretary to bring him coffee just because she's a woman. He expects her to bring him coffee because *he* was born here and she wasn't.

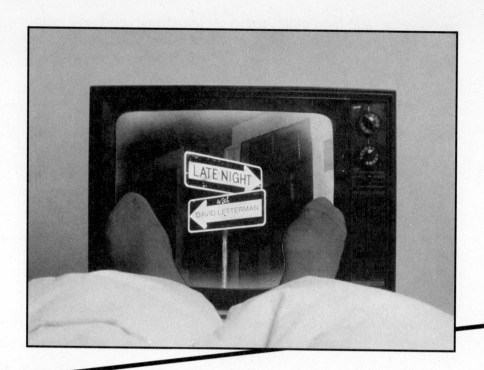

TV Quiz

We know television gives so much and asks so little. The least we as responsible viewers can do is stay informed and up-to-date. With that in mind, we've prepared a little quiz on the television season. If you score less than 50, maybe you ought to take a serious look at your viewing habits.

In *Bonanza,* and then *Little House on the Prairie,* and now *Highway to Heaven,* the one constant element in Michael Landon's television performances has been:

A. his boyish charm
B. his manly courage
C. his girlish bouffant

What is the *major* difference between the shows *The Twilight Zone* and *Silver Spoons*?

A. *The Twilight Zone* had a new cast each week
B. a host introduced each episode of *The Twilight Zone*
C. *The Twilight Zone only occasionally* featured the adventures of hideous mutants

If you were the president of NBC, what would you schedule opposite *Dynasty*?

A. a fast-paced comedy
B. a two-fisted drama
C. a tax write-off

Which of these themes should NBC choose as the subject for a weeklong miniseries?

A. Bismarck's Germany
B. Rome in the age of the Caesars
C. the making of the *Sports Illustrated* swimsuit issue

*M*A*S*H*'s profitability in syndication is:

A. due to its tremendous popularity
B. due to its mass saturation
C. just another reason to hate Alan Alda

Children's television programming is designed to:

A. instill positive social attitudes
B. dispel racial stereotypes
C. make sugar-coated cold cereal actually look nutritious

On a sitcom, when a teenager can't get a date for the dance and his best friend suggests they rent a sheik's costume and ask out the prettiest girl in the class, claiming to be Middle Eastern royalty, the reaction he gets is:

A. disgust and dismay
B. a suggestion to see his clergyman
C. "It's kinda crazy, but it just might work"

Summer replacement series are:

A. breezy fun for the whole family
B. energetic newcomers to the entertainment field
C. a tragic waste of the human spirit

The presence of Dick Van Patten on your screen can only mean:

A. hearty family fare
B. pleasant comedy-drama
C. he beat out Tom Bosley for another trash bag commercial

TV insiders credit NBC's climb to #1 to:

A. actor Bill Cosby
B. executive Brandon Tartikoff
C. a pact with Satan

To boost ratings, *NBC Nightly News* with Tom Brokaw has expanded its format to include:

A. more live broadcasts from foreign capitals
B. more satellite interviews with world leaders
C. a street-wise sidekick named "Velvet, the News Dude"

The words "This is not a true-life documentary, but a fictionalized account" must appear before:

A. *Movies of the Week*
B. historical miniseries
C. 9 out of 10 stories done by Geraldo Rivera

New Gift Ideas

You know, since the show first aired we have been proud to share with our viewers literally hundreds of new products introduced by hopeful manufacturers. They all sold well, but some of them went through the roof. Why, they were more like hotcakes than new products, so fast did they sell. In this exciting section, we'll review this elite group of winners—products that are now fixtures in countless American homes.

Airplane Window Slides

For big fun on your next commercial flight, paste these realistic photos over the windows, then sit back and enjoy the excitement. Slides show wing of plane in flames. Stewardesses guaranteed to drop trays. A must for the frequent flier.

Things-That-Will-Spoil-Without-Refrigeration Scarf

This lovely **embroidered scarf** tells wearers what will spoil without refrigeration. Milk, meat, seafood, deviled ham, tuna salad, anything with a mayonnaise base.

The Shriner Wall Clock

Now you can teach Tommy to tell time with the faces of your favorite famous Shriners. What proud parents wouldn't squeal with delight when their little one says, "It's half-past Frank Soobner."

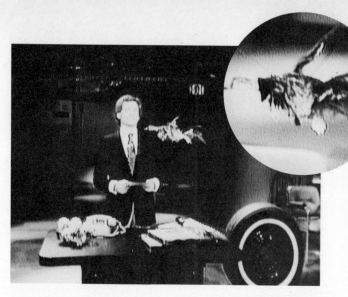

The "Rabid Duck" Party Pooper

Unwanted party stragglers will leave in a hurry when you release this **frightening mechanical bird.** Crazy wind-up mallard flaps madly around room, honking and screeching. Beak snaps wildly. May damage furniture.

"Hangman" Swizzle Stick

"Black Bart" may be a low-down horse thief, but he'll be plumb happy to mix your drink! Realistic and thrilling death throes' action amazes and disgusts party boozers.

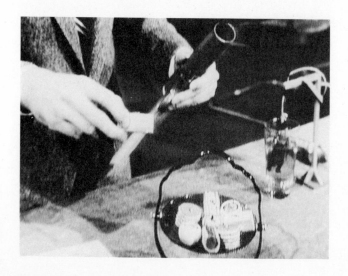

Snack Gun

A new invention that lets you protect yourself without harming attacker. How? By firing a barrage of tasty snacks in his direction. When assailant stoops to pick up delicious hors d'oeuvres, you can escape unharmed. Reloads easily with irresistible smoked salmon and mushroom cartridges.

Zero Gravity Hat

People insure themselves against fire, flood, even earthquakes. But have you ever thought of what would happen to you and your family if *gravity stopped working?* It never has before, but just in case it does, you'll be safe from the head and neck injuries that would result from painful collisions with the ceiling with this **fashionable zero-gravity hat.** After all, aren't you better off safe than sorry!??

Hypno Gas Cap

Remember the days when gas station attendants were really polite and would fill your tank for five bucks? It can still be that way when you turn on the new **hypno gas cap.** In seconds he'll be in a trance and you'll hear things like: "A dollar for twenty-one gallons? Thank you, sir." And "Let me get the *inside* of that windshield too, master."

Depression Mug

At last, a cute **ceramic mug for depressed people**! Bearing the slogan I'D RATHER BE DEAD. Makes a great gift for your suicidal friends.

Line-of-Succession Totem Pole

Never wonder again who's in charge during national emergencies—this clever, **hand-carved totem pole** shows the Constitutional line of succession from President Reagan on down to the Secretary of Agriculture. You'll know at a glance who's running the government. Get one for the car!

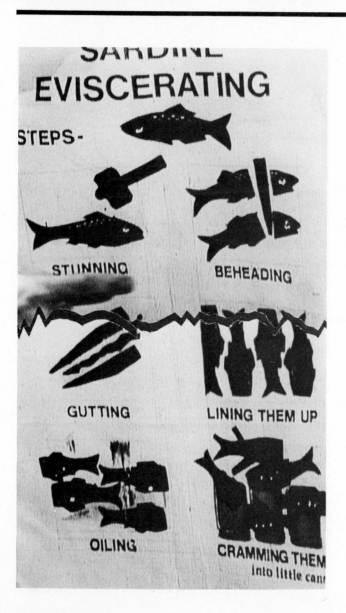

The Sardine Kitchen Tapestry

Depicts steps involved in eviscerating sardines, from ocean to can. Something festive to brighten every kitchen. There's no nicer anniversary gift.

Sloppy Eaters' Tray

When party guests have had a little too much to drink, sometimes those expensive hors d'oeuvres don't quite make it into their mouths. But sloppy eaters won't be a problem when they wear this **new food tray.** After they finish, just snap in this attractive centerpiece, and you have a delightful serving platter full of snacks to serve them when they're hungry later.

Giant Doorknob

In Mexico, it's El Knob Grande. Here in the U.S. we call it **the giant phony doorknob,** and it's a panic. The oversized jumbo knob is much larger than it oughta be—in fact, it's just plain big! Simply attach to an ordinary door and then wait for the fireworks. Your friends will flip when they see how truly big a doorknob can be.

Chopsticks

Old meets new and East meets West in an atmosphere of tolerance and brotherhood. I'm speaking, of course, of these **clever chopstick attachments** for the modern Chinese food lover. Includes fork, knife, spoon, and handy dental mirror.

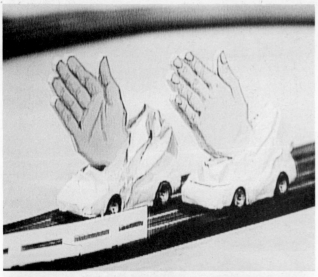

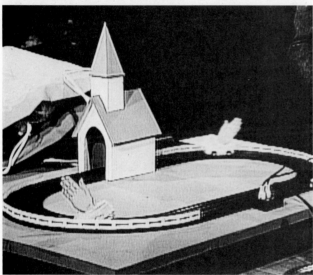

Praying Hands Raceway

Parents know it can be hard to interest their children in faith and religion. But nothing brings out natural reverence in any youngster like the **praying hands raceway**! Albrecht Dürer's masterpiece of devotion is now a thrilling action set, with each hand capable of hitting 80 m.p.h. Sheriff's car not included.

Civil Servant Mug

Here's something for that aunt or uncle who works for the government. This **sassy mug** proudly tells the world, "I'm Dead Wood But They Can't Fire Me." Holds two quarts of coffee, eliminating tiring trips to the coffee pot.

Wacky Meat-Grade Labels

This item is perfect for the summer picnic season. How many times have you said to yourself, "Boy, this church-sponsored cookout sure is dull!" Well, here's something that'll frighten and disgust everyone and give you a laugh at the same time. It's the **wacky meat-grade labels.** Just press onto a few steaks and wait for the frenzy of laughter.

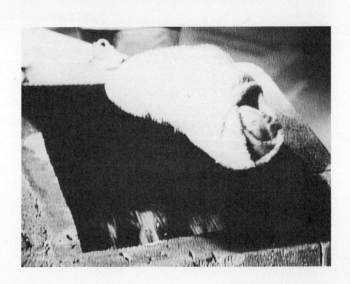

Orphan Alarm

These days, more and more people are awakening to find an unwanted baby on their doorstep—don't you be the next. The **new orphan alarm** lets out a screeching siren whenever a small bundle is placed on it. Then it turns on lawn sprinklers and begins spinning and bucking like an angry bronco. Even irresponsible mothers will try to find a different home for their infant.

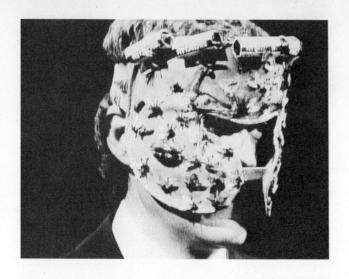

The Flypaper Head Mask

Enjoy those summer picnics and barbecues without the bother of pesky flying insects. Doesn't cover your mouth, so you can eat with ease. Holds up to 2,000 flies or 500 moths.

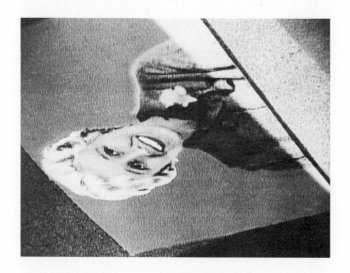

Mom Doormat

Remember how when you were growing up, Mom always said, "You kids treat me like a doormat"? Well, now she *is one,* and she'll remind you to wipe your feet every time you walk in. Yes, it's a laminated photo of *your* mom on a **durable, scuff-resistant plastic doormat.** And her nose works as a gum scraper!

Li'l Archaeologist Kit

The boring TV dinner becomes an educational science project for your kids with this dinner-table anatomy set. Restless youngsters can reconstruct a **complete chicken skeleton** from leftover bones while others finish eating. Includes model glue, construction diagram, and customizing decals.

Turkey Holder

Only a lucky few have three hands—but that's what you need to carve a turkey properly! *Unless* you have one of these new **turkey helmets.** The pronged extension anchors the turkey firmly to the table as the acrylic shield protects you from spattering grease. You won't want to take it off!

Lotion-in-a-Drawer

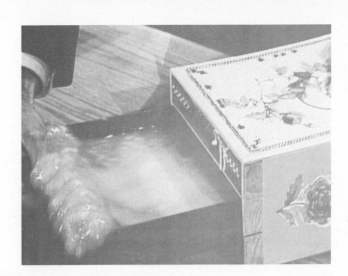

For centuries, women have known that nothing smoothes and softens skin like lotion. But there's always that puzzling problem of how to *store* the messy stuff. Here's the perfect answer—new **lotion-in-a-drawer.** It's all at your fingertips—lotion, oil, and cream.

Dead Guy Rug

Let's face it: very few throw rugs make any sort of comment on our society. But this one is different —it's the **victim outline rug . . . .** Without preaching, this all-nylon carpet will gently remind your guests: "Please, people—let's do something about violent crime."

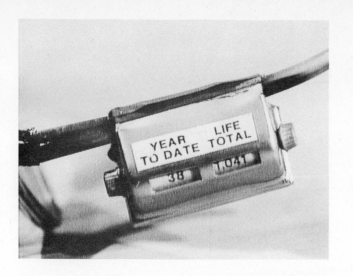

Life-Expectancy Reminder

Based on actuarial tables, this handsome digital timepiece pendant is individually set to remind the recipient how much time he has left to live if everything goes well. Second hand ticks loudly to serve as a constant reminder to every man that time is running out.

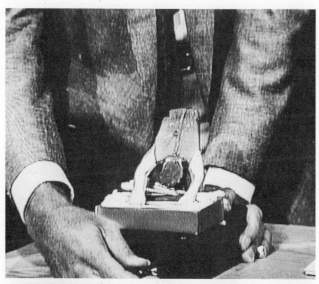

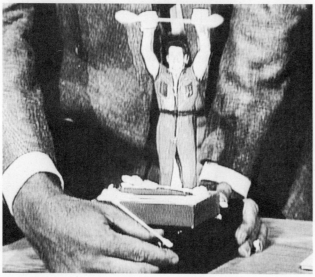

Jack LaLanne Q-Tip Dispenser

Some things just seem to go together—soup and sandwich, brushing and flossing, and now Jack LaLanne and ear hygiene. That's right, it's the **Jack LaLanne Q-Tip dispenser.** So gosh darn cute you'll want to scream.

Cheap Floozy Dolls

Collectors are excited by this new international doll set . . . the limited-edition **Cheap Floozies of the World.** Look at the beautiful hand-crafted detail in each doll. . . .

The U.S.A.'s Carnival Midway Girl
The Hong Kong Bar-Fly
The Amsterdam Novelty Shop Clerk
and the Jet Set's own St. Tropez Trash

Display them with pride—they're sure to become family heirlooms.

Suicide Organizer

Killing yourself—or just thinking about it? This smart **molded-plastic suicide organizer** keeps things neat for whoever finds you. Includes spaces for gun, will, car keys, deposit bottles, and special check-off suicide note. Eliminates that nagging "have I forgotten something" feeling.

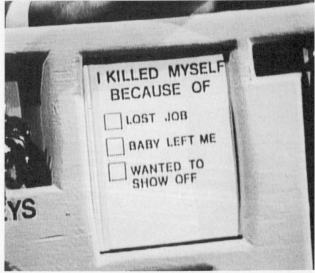

Cereal-Box Battering Ram

Have you always liked those little cereal boxes that fold out to make their own bowl but found they can be a real pain to open? The only *right* way to do it is with this **mini-cereal-box battering ram.** You won't use it often, but when you do—it's a life saver.

Facial Awning

A sun visor is terrific as long as the sun is out, but when it gets cloudy, that visor is just an irritating nuisance. The logical all-weather improvement? The **facial awning.** When the sky turns dark, simply crank it back out of the way.

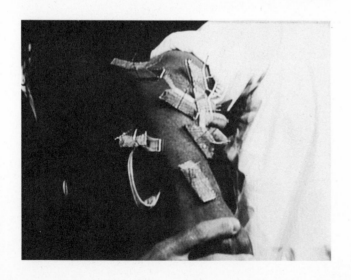

Mosquito Traps

Sure, mosquitoes can be annoying. But that's no reason to *kill* them. Especially when it's so easy to catch them unharmed in these **have-a-heart humane mosquito traps.** When all the cages are full, simply release them in the nearest insect preserve.

Ham Grips

From the people who brought you those cute little corn cob holders, here's a new way to eat lots and lots of ham. With these **whimsical ham grips,** you can polish off an entire canned ham without the embarrassment of greasy fingers.

The Muffin Mortar

Blueberry, bran, or corn—nothing brightens up a morning like the fresh-baked goodness of hot muffins. But passing them to other people at the table is just an irritating distraction. At last you can put an end to breakfast bending with this—**the muffin mortar.**

Ultimate Rubber Glove

Sports fans all across the country love to shout "We're number one." Well, we can't all be number one. And before you can really improve, you've got to face reality and admit you need help. That's the high-scoring idea behind the **We're number 17 giant foam glove.** It's what all really honest fans will be wearing at every big game.

Fly Feeder

Here's just the thing for apartment dwellers and lonely invalids who can't keep pets: the **fly feeder.** Just fill the tray with carrion or rotting fruit, and in no time the room will be filled with cheerful buzzing. Children will enjoy watching the miracle of birth. You'll want several.

Liz Taylor's Ex-Husbands Versus Warren Beatty's Ex-Girlfriends Chess Set

Here's a beautifully crafted collector's item that's sure to please history buffs and gossipmongers alike. . . . It's the **Liz Taylor's ex-husbands versus Warren Beatty's ex-girlfriends chess set**—a new piece arrives by mail every month. What better way to say "I have no taste whatsoever."

Horrid Lawn Gnomes

It's about time Americans faced up to the question "Why should lawn ornaments be simply ornamental?" Well, now unwanted guests and bothersome neighbors will pass your house by when they see these fellows out front—**the horrid, horrid lawn gnomes**. . . . There's nothing to like about them—except the way they work!

The Late Night Viewer: A Profile

Recently, as part of its unceasing effort to improve its programming, NBC commissioned a study aimed at finding out just what sort of person watches our program every night. Although the entire 600-page report is far too voluminous to go into here, it did reveal some fascinating information about the average viewer of *Late Night*. I thought it might be interesting to show you a brief profile of this typical viewer. You may be a little surprised, as I was.

Residence

Nonviewer—split-level three bedroom house.

 Viewer—allowed to use equipment shed at a driving range.

Employment

Nonviewer—insurance sales representative.

 Viewer—no job as such, but sold two Bowie tickets for $150.

Military Service

Nonviewer—two years' weekend service, U.S. Army Reserve.

 Viewer—saw *Stripes*.

Automobile

Nonviewer—1981 Plymouth Reliant.

 Viewer—three motorcycles parked on lawn.

Education

Nonviewer—bachelor's degree, Kansas State University.

 Viewer—would have high school diploma if shop teacher wasn't such a liar.

Marital Status

Nonviewer—married, with two children.

 Viewer—divorced, but would like to get divorced again some day.

Attitude Toward *Entertainment Tonight's* Mary Hart

Nonviewer—can't abide her.

 Viewer—can't abide her.

Awards Won

Nonviewer—children's hospital "Good Samaritan" award.

    Viewer—Twelfth Prize in Publishers' Clearing House Sweepstakes (Aladdin tartan-plaid Thermos).

Preferred Alcoholic Beverage

Nonviewer—blended Irish whiskey.

    Viewer—75-cent well drinks.

Attitude Toward Movies in Which Cycle Gangs Terrorize Ordinary Folks

Nonviewer—repulsed by them.

    Viewer—seeks them out.

Favorite Hobby

Nonviewer—restoring antique wood furniture.

    Viewer—shooting at stop signs with a pellet gun.

Last Major Purchase

Nonviewer—5-h.p. Lawn Boy riding mower.

    Viewer—two 10-pound bags of ice.

Political Affiliation

Nonviewer—last voted Republican ticket in '82 election.

    Viewer—last voted in *US* magazine "Who's Hot—Who's Not" poll.

Audience Etiquette

Every day, hundreds of people from all over the world come to NBC to sit in our studio audience. It's occurred to us recently that most of these people, although they mean well, have never been to a television studio before and are not fully aware of the proper rules of behavior. We thought we'd take this opportunity to give everyone a few friendly pointers.

As a member of the studio audience, you are *a guest*. And because you are a guest, it is in bad taste to watch another show while we are doing this one. Which brings us to Rule #1: When you're in our audience, watch *our* show, or watch nothing at all.

One of the most important jobs you have as an audience member is to keep an eye on the electronic signs above you. They will tell you exactly what is expected of you during the show.

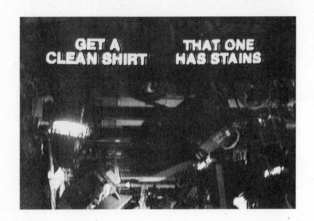

Of course, once the show begins, each and every audience member is entitled to all he can eat from our complimentary buffet. This man has ordered seconds on the blueberry waffles, the chicken fried steak, the tater-tot platter, and the double tequilas. Remember: overweight viewers may be subjected to ridicule during or after the broadcast.

Now, suppose I'm interviewing a guest you like. As an audience member, can you suggest some questions?

Yes, by using the small microphone that is a direct line to me. When I appear to be drinking coffee, I'm actually trying to get to as many audience questions as possible.

Here's another common problem for members of our audience—what to do if your view is blocked by an insensitive cameraman. First, don't panic. There's no reason to get upset. On the floor under your seat

is your personal cameraman prod. It emits a harmless low-voltage jolt that will get even the most hardened cameraman out of your way.

Now a word about the show itself. Some of the humor is very conceptual. A lot of people just don't get it. If this should happen to you, don't be embarrassed to use your complimentary headphones. They will con-

nect you to a team of translators working backstage who will explain each and every joke in simple, easy-to-understand language.

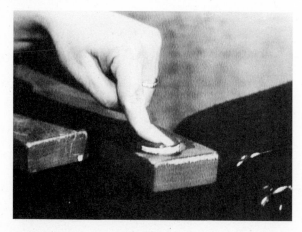

Which brings us to a final important question: What do you do if the guest says something that really, truly offends you? Is there any recourse? Yes. Every

seat is equipped with a red button on the arm. This is the guest-ejector button and should be used only in real emergencies.

How to Be a Responsible TV Viewer

Lately I've been hearing a lot of complaints about how watching TV is a passive entertainment that requires no thinking and how it's turning us into a nation of zombies. I don't think that's fair. Sure, many people don't watch TV responsibly, but that's because they've never learned *how*. The problem with critics who think there's nothing but junk on TV is that they don't watch enough of it. So with this in mind, here are some tips to help you become a more responsible TV viewer.

Now, this man is going about it all wrong—he's procrastinating. He's getting bogged down, paying bills while valuable viewing hours are slipping away (before he even turns on his set).

What you *should* do is turn on the set as soon as you get home. You've got six to eight hours of TV to enjoy —get a move on!

Now, at this point many of you will say: "Sure, watching TV is important, but I don't have the time." Damn it, make the time.

This woman is doing something wrong. She's talking on the phone while watching TV. Don't use the television as a background prop—it's not.

Give television your undivided attention. Don't let a phone call interfere with your TV viewing. Let them hold on the line. You've made a commitment to watch something—honor it.

Here's a rude family. Ignoring each other, their noses buried in books and newspapers—they act as if they're total strangers.

This is more like it: a family working together. And here's good news for everybody: eight hours of TV viewing a night gives you plenty to talk about the next day with friends, teachers, and fellow employees.

Young people often make the mistake of "tuning out" a show just because it's a rerun they've seen before.

What they *should* do is watch it again and take notes. Often you miss things the first time you view a show. Compare your notes with the notes you took the first time you watched. Do you feel differently? How are the characters like people you've met before on other TV shows? You're young, and you've still got a lot of the world left to see. So watch TV—as often and as hard as you can.

Let the others sit through a long movie in a theater while you enjoy one edited for television.

Don't be misled by so-called friends who reject TV in favor of going out.

If you fail to complete the work that was asked of you at the office, level with your boss. Tell him "I couldn't do it. I was watching TV."

He'll admire your style. It might even shake him into becoming a more responsible television viewer himself.

Finally, don't be embarrassed about watching TV. It's more than your right; it's your responsibility. Defend it.
Don't let the world of TV pass you by. Get involved.

Summer Quiz

You know summer is short and you don't want to squander a single moment. But just how well prepared are you for this year's summer fun? Here's your chance to find out, with this convenient summer fun quiz. . . .

The main thing to remember if your picnic is disrupted by a thunderstorm is:

A. don't stand under a tall tree
B. throw yourself flat on the ground
C. make someone else hold the weenie fork

Which fan-appreciation day will draw the largest crowd to Yankee Stadium this summer?

A. bat night
B. helmet night
C. grain-alcohol night

What is the official first day of summer?

A. June 21
B. the summer solstice
C. the day George Steinbrenner fires the Yankees' manager

What is the biggest safety hazard on the beach?

A. perilous undertow
B. muscle cramps while swimming
C. asking someone who wasn't born in this country to turn down his radio

If President Reagan were to choose one summer activity, it would be:

A. going horseback riding
B. chopping wood
C. the first decision he's made for himself since taking office

Who could swim farther out into the ocean without drowning: Julio Iglesias or Steve Lawrence?

A. Julio Iglesias
B. Steve Lawrence
C. hard to say, but it's definitely worth trying

What is the most common summer pest?

A. mosquitoes
B. horseflies
C. TV commercials set to Beach Boys music

What should be your signal for leaving the beach?

A. thunderclouds
B. dry, burning skin
C. the fat couple next to you has completed foreplay

Dave's Toy Shop

Anyone who's shopped for a youngster has met with the frustration of finding all the most popular toys sold out. Oddly enough, this is never a problem with these new playthings. For some reason they are always available in large quantities. Here, for the young and just the young-at-heart, are some favorite offerings from "Dave's Toy Shop."

Wiffle Ax

It's a known fact that every now and then all children harbor deep feelings of hostility toward the human race, feelings that just aren't healthy for a growing tot. Well, that's no longer a problem, thanks to the new **Wiffle Ax**! Yes, at long last, the same wonderful Wiffle technology that made living room sports safe now does the same thing for mindless acts of childhood violence.

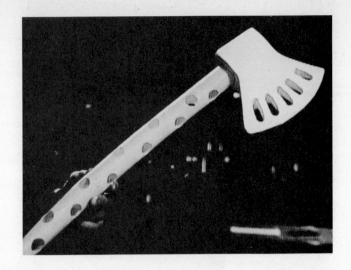

Gandhi Bag

Here's a progressive toy—it's the **Mahatma Gandhi Passive Resistance Punching Bag.** While youngsters pound away at the Hindu man of peace, he'll be teaching them a lesson in the futility of violence. Mahatma Gandhi—pacifist or just plain yellow? You be the judge.

Barbie's Parking Space

Here's something every Barbie fan will want—it's **Barbie's Parking Space.** Little girls can have hours of educational fun helping Barbie park, pull out, and then park again. Doll and convertible purchased separately. At a recent convention, this was voted "Toy of the Year" for 1985.

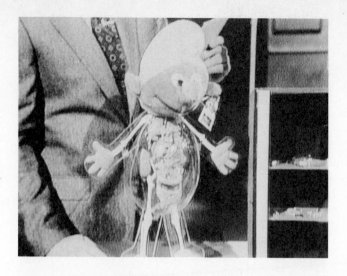

Visible Smurf

This year, the Smurfs have stolen the hearts of countless children. Now, for the science-minded youngster, there's new **Visible Smurf.** The clear plastic abdomen reveals all the major organ groups as well as the oxygen-starved blood that makes the Smurfs do those silly stunts.

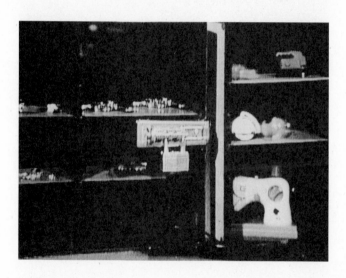

Li'l Pawnbroker

Hard economic times can present tough career choices to young people. With the **Li'l Pawnbroker Set,** kids learn that the financial suffering of others can be a real bonanza to them. Comes complete with pawn tickets, glass case, shotgun—everything they'll need to become scavengers of human misery.

Big-City Bus Depot

Here's an action play set that's every bit as fun as anything from Lionel . . . it's the 105-piece **Big-City Bus Depot.** Let your child enter the magic world of runaways and weirdos! From the derelicts and the con artists out front to the busted vending machines along the wall—it's all here! And open twenty-four hours a day for round-the-clock fun!

Sensible Putty

Boys and girls can waste hours playing with Silly Putty, having fun but accomplishing nothing. This new toy, **Sensible Putty,** may not bounce, but it's just what your son or daughter needs to practice bathroom caulking and window sealing. Let other kids throw their lives away peeling up the pictures from comic strips. Your kids' future is in this container.

Infant Gravity Booties

Now you can be sure that your infant won't get into trouble or develop back problems while you're busy, thanks to these brand-new high-quality **Infant Gravity Booties.** Hang Junior up while you're cooking or on the phone, and you'll come back to a taller, happier baby.

Subway Etiquette

To the native New Yorker who rides the subway system several times a day, the phrase "subway etiquette" may seem to be a contradiction in terms. But that didn't stop us from using it as a premise for the following piece.

Before entering the subway, take a few wise precautions. If you have to carry valuables, always use a bag like this.

Next you will pass through a metal detector. This sounds a warning if you do not have enough metal, indicating that you are insufficiently armed for subway travel.

Once you are safely on board, it is customary to introduce yourself to everyone in the car by announcing your name and destination.

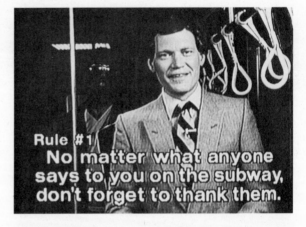

This is an example of a subway faux pas.

As with all forms of travel, choosing the proper seat is of paramount importance. So don't be afraid to be fussy. Review each seat individually. Is it pleasing to the eye? Would you prefer an aisle or a window?

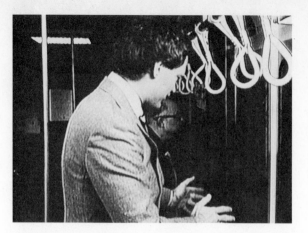

A happy traveler knows what he wants and refuses to settle for second best.

Here's something that's fun to do on a subway car. Put together your own little chemistry set like I've done here. This will enable you to identify all the peculiar things you find around you on the seats and walls when you travel.

For example, here's something I collected from the back of the seat in front of me. It turned out to be saliva, human hair, chewing gum, and pickle relish. To my way of thinking, it could have been so much worse.

Here's a common subway etiquette problem: In the event a bum passes out on you, what is the polite thing to do?

Rule #3
FRESHEN UP A
SLEEPING BUM

Take the opportunity to help him freshen up. He'll thank you when he awakens.

You're also going to want to spend some time hanging on to these straps like the real New York subway riders do.

It'll give you a chance to study some really interesting people at close range. Which brings us to another common problem: What is the proper behavior for dealing with someone who is talking to his- or herself?

Listen politely, offering small rejoinders where appropriate, such as "Mmmmhmmm" and "I understand" or "No kidding."

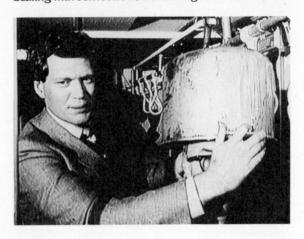

Then offer him one of these specially designed microwave protector helmets, which will not only fend off the dangerous Russian mind-control lasers that are beamed at us day after day but will muffle his conversation so you can ride in peace.

Then refer him to one of our talent coordinators so we can book him on the show.

Dave's Video Funhouse

Dust off your thinking caps, folks. It's time for yet another stimulating compendium of riddles, puzzles, and paradoxes from the fascinating world of show business. Yes, it's a chance to take another look at some of the brain teasers we like to call "Dave's Video Funhouse."

Search-and-see puzzle:
    Can you find Grace Jones hidden among all these
anvils, irons, and aircraft carriers?

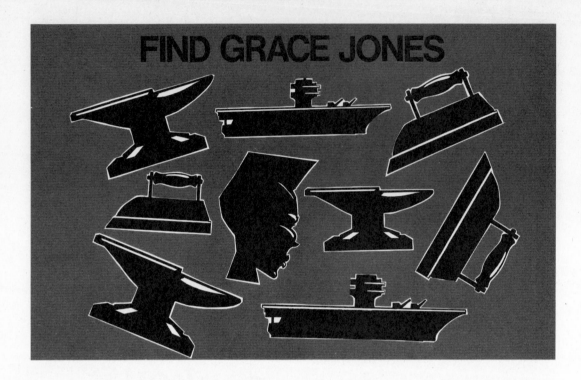

If Liza Minnelli receives rave reviews from 85 percent
of New York's 34 theater critics, what does she have?

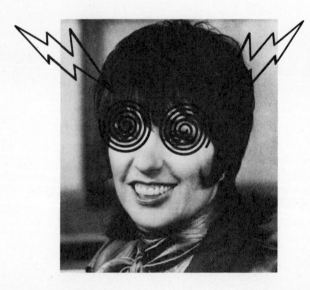

The eerie power to cloud men's minds.

Here's an optical illusion: Is House Speaker Tip O'Neill
wider than he is tall?

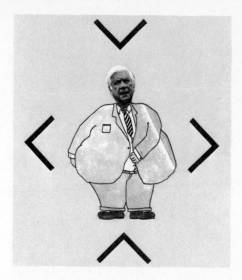 

Actually, this is a trick question. Tip only *seems*
wide because he's stuffed his jacket full of complimentary danish from the pages' lounge.

What do the critics generally regard as Pia Zadora's
greatest emotional strength as an actress?

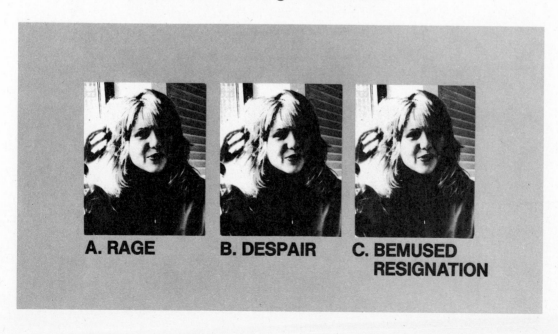

A. RAGE   B. DESPAIR   C. BEMUSED
                                    RESIGNATION

Match the periodical with its proudest journalistic achievement.

The Washington Post — UNCOVERING THE WATERGATE SCANDAL

NATIONAL REVIEW — SPECIAL ISSUE ON THE IMPACT OF VIETNAM

Us — RATING THE CELEBRITY SUPERBODIES

What was the happiest day in Marlo Thomas' life?
A. the day *That Girl* debuted
B. the day she met Phil Donahue
C. the day she found out she didn't have to keep her father's nose all of her life

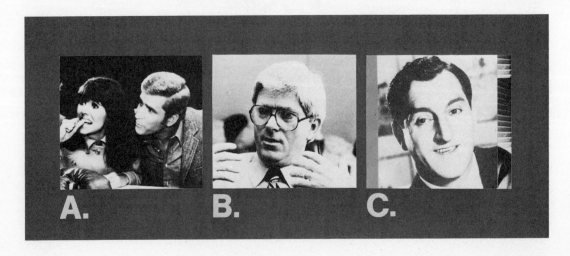

A.   B.   C.

Here's a game for folks who subscribe to both *U.S. News & World Report* and *People* magazine: match the emerging African nation with its favorite form of government *and* the TV starlet with her favorite color.

If Ricky Schroder and Gary Coleman had a fight on television with pool cues, who would win?

A. Ricky Schroder
B. Gary Coleman
C. The television viewing public

Which of the following are *not* marsupials?

A. an opossum mother and her young
B. a kangaroo mother and her offspring
C. Michael Jackson and Emmanuel Lewis

Here's a search-and-see puzzle. You have five seconds. Can you find Marlon Brando in this group of Mr. Potato Heads?

FIND MARLON BRANDO

Which number is the smallest?
A. the number of states in the U.S. in 1812
B. the number of revolutions the earth makes in
    a month
C. the number of English-speaking cab drivers in
    New York

Here's a puzzle you won't have to set aside the whole afternoon for: connect the dots and you'll see Prince's mustache.

Here's an optical illusion:
　　What do you see here, a very fragile, hand-cut crystal goblet or silhouettes of Barbra Streisand and Barry Manilow?

Based on what you've read about him in history books, what do you think Abraham Lincoln would be doing if he were alive today?

Writing his memoirs of the Civil War.

Advising the President.

Desperately clawing at the inside of his coffin.

Which of the following requires the most daily maintenance work?
A. a Boeing 747 jumbo jet
B. the Grand Coulee Dam
C. Joan Collins

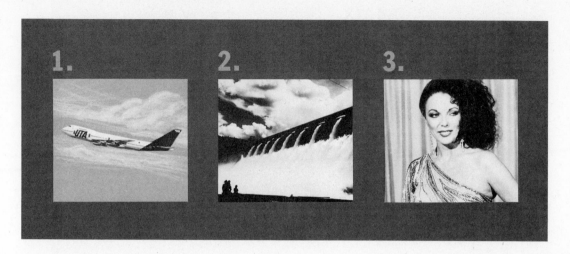

Andy Rooney has done an exasperatingly pointless essay on every one of them.

Match the movie to Elvis' occupation in it.

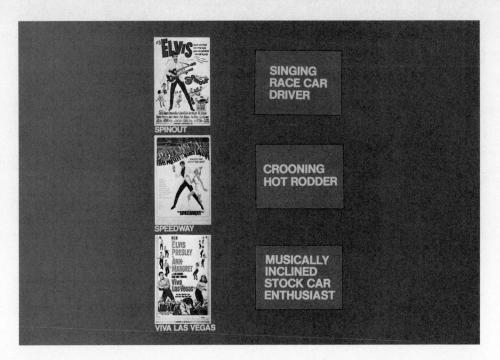

Here's a problem that tests your ability to navigate some pretty treacherous social waters. You are the producers of *Night of 100 Stars*. You've just signed your ninety-ninth star when the Gabor sisters unexpectedly drop by your office. What should you do?

A.   choose Zsa-Zsa
B.   choose Eva
C.   change the name of the show to *Night of 99 Stars*

The World of the Future

The technology being developed in today's research labs is going to affect all of us. Life in the world of tomorrow will certainly be challenging and maybe even a little scary. That's why we'd like to give you a brief look at some of the things you can expect to see in . . . the world of the future.

In the future, ordinary haircuts will be obsolete. Instead, you'll wear this haircut monitor, which will sound an ear-splitting siren when your hair reaches a preset length. Designed to be worn at all times, it will weigh no more than a portable typewriter.

If you ignore the siren, tiny laser torches will burn off the excess hair. No more inconvenient haircut appointments.

Here's another engineering breakthrough, the **long-range thermometer.** It'll allow you to measure body temperatures up to 600 miles away.

Is the lead singer in your favorite band running a fever? You'll know in seconds.

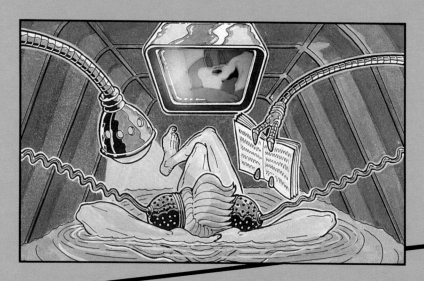

Today, when you get into a sensory deprivation tank, it's dark, isolated, and boring. After several minutes your mind starts to wander. But in a few years, deluxe models will be available complete with built-in stereo, telephone, and reading lamp to occupy you during those tedious hours of seclusion.

Youngsters of the future will be bored with today's
chemistry sets. New science kits like this one will ex-
plore exciting areas like "the world of animal DNA."
Kids will love playing with the "building blocks" of
life. This set will include hypodermic syringes and
22 kinds of DNA.

They'll also get an idea booklet for creating strange
pets.

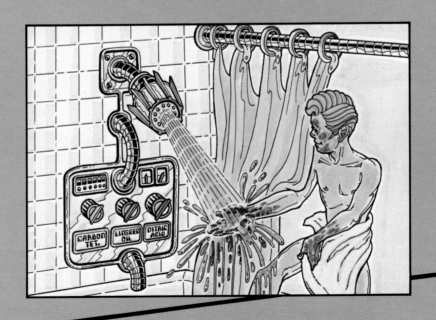

Even your bathroom shower will have a new look.
Instead of just plain water, you'll have a choice of
industrial solvents for those really *tough* wash-up
jobs. Select from carbon tetrachloride, linseed oil,
or nitric acid sprays.

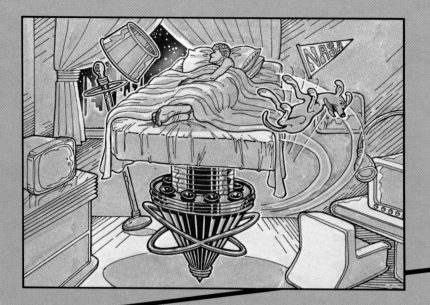

This magnetic swivel mattress, now being developed, will turn your bed into a huge but very sensitve compass. Your body will always point true north, no matter what the earth does. Not even major avalanches or sunspots can divert your head from the North Pole.

The science of large-scale cloning will finally bring identical copies of America's best-loved entertainers into every home. Why have a dull housekeeper when a thrilling Las Vegas performer like Robert Goulet can sing for your family twenty-four hours a day?

Camping with Barry White

Camping with Barry White can be a sublime experience, or it can be a nightmare. It depends on your attitude and, frankly, on having the proper equipment. We went to Barry himself for his list of indispensable camping utensils, and this is what he recommended.

According to Barry White, when you're looking for a sleeping bag, look for three things: it should be round, it should have a mirrored ceiling attachment, and it should have magic-finger massage action. Not surprisingly, the official Barry White model passes all these tests.

When Barry White lounges around the campsite, he does it like he does everything else—in style, but with a respect for the environment. These **satin lounging pajamas** in dappled shades of camouflage blend in beautifully with the surrounding underbrush.

For a truly sensual massage, warm oil is a necessity, but in some campsites, firewood can be scarce. That's why Barry developed this **solar massage oil warmer.** A few minutes of sunlight will bring you hours of sensuous bliss after dark.

You can't go camping without cooking utensils, but there's no law that says they can't be stylish. This **solid gold mess-kit ring** lets Barry White's fingers sparkle and also allows him to fry up fish and small game.

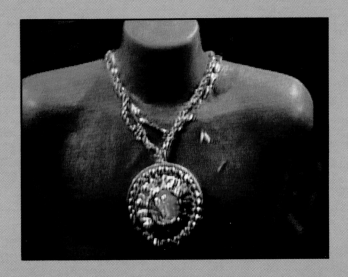

This gold medallion is more than a handsome piece of jewelry. It's also an **ultraviolet bug lamp** that zaps mosquitoes with 600 volts of electricity. You look like a million, and your campsite's free of flying insects.

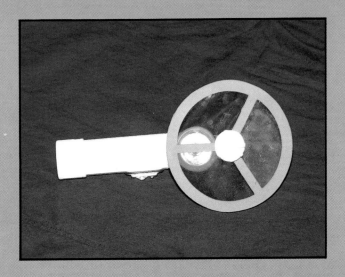

Whether he's singing on a concert stage or camping in a remote wilderness, Barry likes to create a special atmosphere. This custom-designed **mood flashlight** softly bathes even the darkest forest in the rich colors of love.

Back-to-School Quiz

September sneaks up on us before we know it—and then it's time to make that tough transition from dozing away your days on a balmy beach to dozing away your days in a noisy classroom. To help prepare you for the change of seasons, we've designed our back-to-school quiz.

What aspect of public education has not changed in fifty years?

A. overcrowded classrooms
B. low teachers' salaries
C. gelatin desserts in unnatural colors

To instill confidence, a shop teacher should have:

A. skill as a draftsman
B. a working knowledge of all power tools
C. most of his fingers

Students preparing for a career in the auto industry should study:

A. math and science
B. engineering
C. Japanese

This fall, students in the army R.O.T.C. program will review:

A. parade ground drills
B. proper care of dress uniforms
C. maps of Nicaragua

Which great man do most high school principals resemble?

A. George Washington
B. George Steinbrenner
C. George Gobel

At universities with big-time sports programs, student-athletes are seldom seen:

A. breaking curfew
B. smoking cigarettes
C. in class

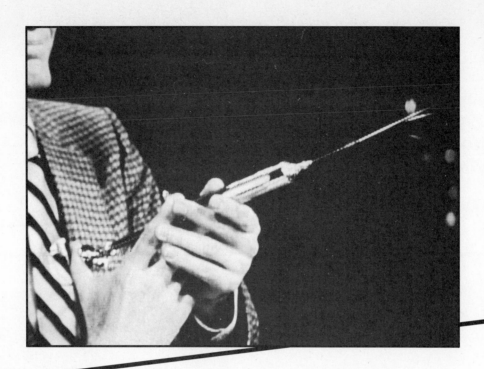

New Medical Aids

In recent years, the world of medicine has seen an exponential increase in new technological devices and gadgetry...a surprising number of which have turned out to be slipshod and suspect. What follows are some of the American Medical Association's attempts to cash in on the public's voracious appetite for more novelty items, even in so delicate an area as personal health.

Combination Spit-Sink and Aquarium

Now an otherwise depressing spit-sink is also a cherished pet.

Walter Cronkite Surgical Mask

Thanks to this simple disguise, all patients can now have the peace of mind that comes with being operated on by the most trusted man in America.

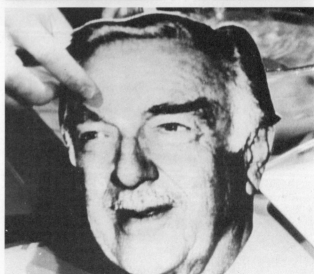

Lifetime Glasses

These remarkable glasses let you update lens prescriptions yourself as your eyes change. Never go to the eye doctor again!

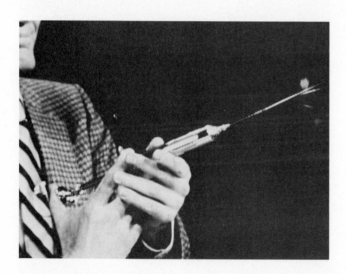

Hypodermic Noisemaker

Allows each painful injection to be accompanied by the sound of a loudly moaning cow.

Lifelike Duplicates of Internal Organs

Perfect for recovery room pranks. Leave one of these in someone's bed, and he'll momentarily believe that the doctor forgot to put something back. Also available in kidneys, spleen, et cetera.

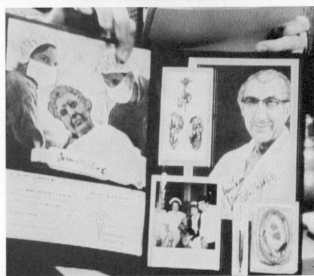

Operation Scrapbook

Medical memories will be preserved forever in this beautiful cowhide-bound album. Contains spaces for lab reports, doctor autographs, and, of course, surgical specimens. Remember your big day in style.

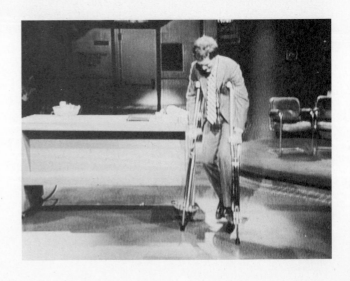

Pogo Crutches

Really let you cover ground, even with a serious injury.

Hotel Etiquette

There's a certain kind of person who likes to do things right. They eat at five-star restaurants, drive expensive cars, vacation at posh resorts, and often own more than one riding mower. (No one knows why they want more than one. They are rich and powerful, and we simply accept their eccentricities.) That kind of person leads a challenging and rewarding life that seldom includes *Late Night* television viewing. And we don't give a damn about *them*, either. No, it's for *you*—the drifter, the wastrel, the guy with lots and lots of time on his hands—that we went all the way to the Virgin Islands to tape the following report.

The seasoned traveler makes sure to read *everything* in his quest for a bargain. The sign on the door to the room is a perfect example of what I mean.

Winter season rates: *One* person stays in this room for $196. *Two* persons for *$198*. So it's a good idea to hang around the lobby until you find someone who already *has* a room. Then give him the extra two bucks, and you can stay with him!!

Here we are in the bathroom, and we see more informative signs.

"All room towels are accounted for. Please do not remove from your room."

If you're anything like me, this is *not* a problem. You're here to load up on bedspreads and pillowcases.

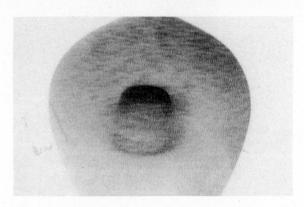

Before you come to the Virgin Islands, everyone tells you, "Wait until you see the water. It's unbelievably blue." As you can see, they're absolutely right. It's just like in the postcards.

Your hotel phone is marked with a variety of different extensions so you can call and get anything you need. Right after you check in, *be sure and ring each one* just to let them know that you're here.

There is no end to the fun you can have.

"Hello? Room service? Send up a room." No one ever tires of a *really* good joke, so you'll want to play this one often.

Here's a handy tip: Your room key has postage guaranteed. So you can use it as a stamp.

Just attach any personal mail to your key, and tell your friends to pick up their letters at the hotel desk.

Which brings us to the topic of Free Hotel Gifts. Every hotel room comes equipped with a *complimentary piece of lawn furniture*. Don't forget to take yours with you when you check out.

And take a look at this TV. For your convenience, finer hotels don't even bolt them to the floor. You can have that baby out of there in no time.

There's no more common traveler's dilemma than this classic packing problem: if you put the bedspreads and pillowcases into the suitcase first, where will you ever find room to put the lamp?

That's why the wise traveler remembers to *bring along more than one suitcase*. Otherwise, you might have to make several trips.

One other thing that makes hotels the greatest places on earth—free ice and more free ice! You're entitled to all you can carry! Be sure to get your fair share.

And leave plenty of room in your suitcase to take any extra back home with you. I have found there's really nothing quite like it for everything from cooling drinks to packing fish.

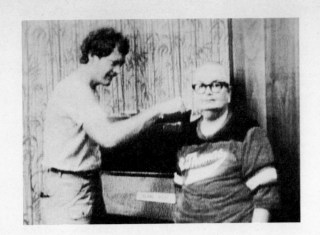

Let's Meet the Writers!

by Jeff Martin

Much as I love writing for *Late Night* and tending to Dave's laundry needs, I've always felt that something was missing in the show's relationship with its audience. Though the bond between TV writer and TV viewer in many ways goes far deeper than that between husband and wife, we don't really *know* each other.

This problem came to my attention recently when I visited a local high school to talk to the kids, help them work out their problems, and dispense grooming tips. The young people were struck by how different I was from the conception they had formed from seeing my name in the credits. Some had thought I was Oriental. Others couldn't get over how tall I was. A stupid fat guy with no friends had thought I was a woman.

By the end of the evening, my mission for this book had become clear: the *Late Night* writers and their audience must be *strangers no more*. Seized with the fury of sudden inspiration, I tore up my first, much funnier essay, and wrote this one.

Let's Meet the Writers:

Dreamy **SANDY FRANK** is the sort of fellow your parents curse at you for not being like. Blond. Handsome. Tall. Short. Sandy shares an office with **JOSEPH E. TOPLYN**, whose swinging, anything-for-a-kick personality has earned him the colorful nickname "Joe."

STEVE O'DONNELL has also picked up a (in this case, meaningless) nickname: "Head Writer." Though he is more often than not a burnout victim, Steve's face still lights up at the sight of a well-tuned joke written on a crisp twenty-dollar bill.

FRED GRAVER and **KEVIN CURRAN** are a couple of regular guys, and their frequent sojourns to the local pub for "just one more" drink and subsequent visits to AA are a standing joke around the office. Though not funny in any sense of the word, their jokes garner high marks for good intentions.

It really boosts office morale to have a "goat" like **RANDY COHEN** we can make the butt of little jokes, such as putting gum on his chair, or slaying a beloved family pet. Randy is understandably a bit sensitive about his father's being in prison, so the less said about that, the better.

Randy's office mate, **LARRY JACOBSON**, is a perfectly adequate writer and his jokes here should go a long way toward dispelling rumors to the contrary. I'm sorry, but that's not my idea of a "loser."

GERRY MULLIGAN has been working for the show a long time—too long, we sometimes joke around the office. At forty years old, Gerry is not so much a productive member of the staff as a beloved father figure.

And I can't even begin to list the virtues of those **WRITERS NEXT DOOR**, whose names seem to have slipped my mind.

We're a varied bunch here at *Late Night,* but we all share one thing: a deep sense of gratitude to our viewers for all the loyalty and support they've given us over the years. We love our work and have no intention of leaving. So quit calling us and asking for jobs, you.

How to Become a Writer for Late Night

by Joseph E. Toplyn

Job vacancies don't crop up very often on the *Late Night* writing staff, but it does happen. So let's say you've been reading this book and thinking to yourself, "Hey, *I* could write this stuff." Well, maybe you could. The question is, what's the best way to parlay whatever talent you have into a cozy spot on our staff?

The answer to that question can be summarized in one word: laugh. Through a remarkable coincidence, each letter in "laugh" stands for a time-tested job hunting tip. Let's take those letters one at a time.

L—Learn the jargon.

We *Late Night* writers use a lot of abbreviations when we talk about the show, to save time and baffle eavesdroppers. For example, we refer to our "New Gift Items" segment as "Wacky Props" or, more familiarly, "Wackies."

Below is a list of our most frequently used abbreviations. Memorize it, then score points by using these expressions in your job application and in your personal interviews with Dave.

Expression	What It Means
Dial-its	Jokes about new telephone dial-it services
Spackies	Jokes about spackling or grouting
Pinheads	Jokes about Larry "Bud" Melman
Hooters	Jokes about owls
Love lumps	Hooters
B. M.	British Museum
Yahoos	Our viewers

A—A Sample of Your Comedy Writing Should Be Sent to the Current Writers for Feedback.

We'll read your material, discuss it, and, if we think it's funny, present it to Dave. (Don't worry. So he won't be prejudiced against it, we'll say we wrote it.)

If Dave gives your material the green light, we'll be sure it gets on the air as part of an actual show. It'll be a terrific learning experience for you. And if that show happens to be nominated for an Emmy, we'll let you know in plenty of time to watch the ceremonies on TV.

By the way, when you're mailing us your material, please enclose a self-addressed, stamped envelope, so we can steam the stamp off it.

U—Understand the Importance of Collaborating with Other Writers.

Why? Because at *Late Night* we've found that the best comedy only happens when several writers, each with a different strength, work together.

For example, here's how the writing chores were divided up on one of our most successful segments ever—"Dave's Hyena Rodeo":

Writer A: Original concept, preliminary treatment, and final script.
Writer B: Worked "tab" key on typewriter.
Writer C: Chuckled appreciatively when idea was described to him.
Writer D: Took credit for idea in interview with *Rolling Stone*

G—Get Going and Write, Write, Write.

The more you write, the easier it'll get, and the better your chances will be of landing a job on the staff. *What* you write doesn't make much difference. Certified checks and money orders are best, but some of us writers will take personal checks too, with three forms of identification.

H—Have a Nice Day.

Maybe this won't actually help you get a job on *Late Night,* but it'll make it easier for you to *pretend* you have one. Besides, I needed an "H" to spell "laugh." Get off my back, will you?

"You Work for Late Night? Can I Ask You Something?"

by Fred Graver

When people hear what I do for a living, there are three questions I am almost invariably asked:

—What's Dave like?
—What's Paul like?
—If your words don't appear anywhere, and if they aren't read by anybody, it's not really writing, is it?

The answers:
—He's nice.
—He's nice.
—It is too, dammit.

Now, in the course of my brief conversations with these same people, they begin to sense the deep and profound wisdom I possess. The experience is not unique to me—all the *Late Night* writers have it. Whatever this quality is that we possess, it's not long after we meet people that we find ourselves plumbing the depths of human experience.

What follows are the real important, deep questions I am most often asked. I can't speak for the other writers—like priests, we are sworn by a sacred vow not to reveal what is said to us in these worldly confessionals.

How About It? You Got Any Hot Stock Tips?

No. None. My financial advice to everyone is: Make a million bucks, and pay cash for everything. After you go through your million, die. I think the world would be greatly improved if everyone was given a million dollars at birth and told, "When you're done with that, you're vapor, pal. No investments, no credit cards. This is it."

When Should My Daughter Begin Dating?

The first date is the most important date of all, and should be undertaken with someone who will be understanding and gentle. There are three or four writers here in the *Late Night* office (myself excluded) who fulfill these requirements.

The parents I talk to often consider this option for their daughter, especially if it means a couple of extra tickets.

I'm Considering a Risky Operation. If the Operation Is Unsuccessful, My Loved Ones and My Professional Colleagues Will Forever Lead Disrupted, Miserable Lives. Should I Get a Second Opinion?

My feeling is this—you don't need the operation if you've still got the energy to seek a second opinion. Get as many opinions as humanly possible. Move like a little metal ball around the spinning roulette wheel of the medical establishment until one day you fall, exhausted, into one doctor's slot. I think if you follow this advice you'll be all right.

How Much Money Do the Recipients of the MacArthur Foundation "Genius Grants" Get?

I really don't know. When they called me, I said, "Keep your money. I'm making a fine living in network television, and getting the best possible opportunity in the world for expressing my creative self. Why don't you give the money to John Sayles?" And they did.

What's Dave Like?

Like I said before, he's nice.

My First Three Months as a Late Night Writer

by Larry Jacobson

Before I lived in New York and wrote for *Late Night,* I lived in Los Angeles and wrote for *Late Night.* A lot of people (especially the other writers on the show) used to wonder how this was possible. It was difficult, to say the least, but I did it. This is a rough outline of what my daily schedule was for the first three months.

September 1984

5 A.M.: Alarm clock goes off. I jump out of bed. Put on my jogging suit. Find my way to my car and begin the journey to the newsstand. I purchase my four daily papers and head back home. It's only six blocks away. But everybody drives everywhere in California.

5:15 A.M.: Time for breakfast. A glass of o.j., cereal, and milk. Sounds pretty healthy. So I top it off with a couple of teaspoons of Häagen-Dazs chocolate chocolate chip ice cream.

5:30 A.M.: Breakfast is over. Now the job begins. I start leafing through the newspapers to find subject matter for the "opening remarks." You know how David says two or three jokes at the top of the show? That's what I was hired to write. Let's see what the good topics are for today. Amtrak, there's been a lot of accidents lately. Hurricane Diana is causing havoc all over the Southeast. And the presidential campaign. Good. I have topics. Now all I need are jokes.

6:15 A.M.: Lunch break. What should I have. Sandwich? Salad? I'll grab a sandwich.

6:30 A.M.: Lunch is over. Back to work.

6:45 A.M.: Coffee break. That's the last break of the day.

6:50 A.M.: Back to work for the final ten minutes.

7:00 A.M.: The phone rings. It means New York is calling. It's ten o'clock back there. I'll let it ring a few more times. Finally I pick it up. It's Ralph, a college intern who works for *Late Night.*

Larry
Hello.

Ralph
Hi, Larry. Ralph. Are you ready?

Larry
Sure. Let's go. Joke number one . . .

Fourteen jokes (or one half hour) later, Ralph reads the jokes back to make sure he has the correct wording. We say our goodbyes.

Ralph
Goodbye, Larry.

Larry
Goodbye, Ralph.

8:00 A.M.: It's 8:00 in the morning and my day's over. What do I do now? I guess I'll catch up on my sleep. Relax. And anxiously await the show that night to see if any of my jokes make the cut.

8:01 A.M. to 12:27 A.M.: Time is split between naps and game shows.

12:28 A.M.: I tune in NBC. I see Carson say good night to Charles Nelson Reilly and Shelley Winters. It's coming up soon.

12:30 A.M.: The music, the opening montage, the Bill Wendell announcement . . . "David Letterman . . ."

David
John Hinckley wants to vote by absentee ballot in the upcoming presidential election. It's nice to see that the guy has stayed so politically involved.

A beat. David looks around. No response from the audience.

David
Was that even a joke? Let's go for number two. Gromyko is visiting New York right now. He went to the Russian Tea Room. And he wasn't wearing a jacket. So they said to him, "I'm sorry, you can't come in here. You don't have a jacket." And he says, "Yes. But I have an accent."

No response. Boy, I'm glad I'm in L.A.

On January 7, 1985, this routine ended when I moved to New York City. Now the only problem is when the jokes don't work, it's so much harder to hide.

Do You Have a Future in Television?

by Kevin Curran

Everyone loves television. From toddler to oldster, there's a special program for each viewer as well as an advertised product on the show that makes life that much more livable. There's also a special magic to television—who among us can forget childhood memories of running outside on a hot summer's eve to the "clang, clang" of the television repair truck's bell?

But television is not a field for children—the equipment is too heavy for them to operate and they are much stupider and slower than adults. No, television is a sacred trust handed down from generation to generation, like the Washington Monument or the odd guy with the hacking cough who was your high school janitor for fifty years.

Is a career in television right for you? It's a very difficult question to answer. First off, are you the cute girl in the pink halter over there, or the geek swilling diet orange soda from the paper bag? Well, never mind —from now on we'll just call you Q.

Q. How should I go about looking for my first television job?

A. An excellent question, Q. Most high-level executives that I know in the industry assure me of one thing: there is nothing they look forward to more than receiving long, whiny letters from people in college looking for jobs. The letters must, of course, attach a great deal of importance to hopes and fears in the students' own lives, as well as making a few tangential forays into their pathetic, uninformed feelings on side issues, such as nuclear disarmament. These twenty or so pages should be followed by a long list of demands for limousines, personal bodyguards, microwave ovens, and other junk, then conclude with a reference to selling your soul to the devil to work in a "vast wasteland."

Q. What's the most important thing I should know about the inner workings of a network?

A. Never go down alone in an elevator with a guy named Gummy. Of this, more I cannot say.

Q. What else?

A. Well, P, I mean, Q, it would probably be wise to familiarize yourself with some common network practices, such as counterprogramming, building a programming strategy in time blocks, and the eerie and mysterious worship of Satan and all his minions.

Q. If I manage to land an interview for my "TV Dream Job," how should I act?

A. A woman should dress in a way that is both conservative and professional. I would recommend either a solid gray or navy blue outfit. At any point after the introductions are made, she should yawn politely, mention that she would like to slip into something comfortable, and return in a short, frilly nightie, holding a pitcher of gimlets and a small cheese-and-cracker platter.

A man should dress in a dark suit and greet his interviewer with a rugged handshake, a warm smile, and 8 × 10 glossies of family members he thinks the interviewer would like to "date."

The manuscript crumbled to dust in my hands. Griddley puffed on the Zalonian pipe he had unearthed last year in the expedition to the jungle world of Pliono.

"How interesting," remarked the world's most illustrious space archaeologist. "It would appear, judging from the material and method of composition, that this document could be dated sometime during the twentieth century on Earth. This was the time of Theodore Roosevelt, Adolf Hitler, Richard Nixon, and, of course, Bonaxo the Greater. Discovering how it made its way to this arid, untutored land light years away will perhaps prove to be our greatest challenge."

I smiled weakly as I watched the image of the planet's double-sun glint in his dark glasses. Soon the poison would paralyze his entire nervous system. His death was on my hands, but what of it. A robot has no feelings.

Especially a robot named: Abraham Lincoln!

A Faceful of Memories

by Steve O'Donnell

What is it like working on *Late Night*? That's a mighty hard question to answer. It's so *many* things . . . a myriad of people and places . . . a kaleidoscope of friends and feelings. . . . It's the sunny smiles of Babs and Jude; the bright lights of Studio 6-A; the ever-fresh excitement when the daily script arrives still warm from the copy service. . . . It's the merry tinkle of the pastry cart every morning at ten; the tantalizing fumes from the Xerox fluid; Dave at the piano for the Wednesday night sing-alongs; the pungent aroma of frying bologna coming from Bill Wendell's dressing room; and everywhere the piles of memorabilia from the Golden Age of Trollies and

Interurbans. . . . It's the fun everybody had during the intern hazing—and the way we all stuck together during the police inquest afterward. . . . It's the blunt, sour smell of chlorine in the locker room, and the muffled booming of the diving board. . . . It's the terrifying whine of the 88-millimeter shells coming down on our heads; the steady clip-clopping of the horses on the cobblestone street below; and the sweet sickly stench of roasting human flesh. . . . It's the quizzical song of the whippoorwill down the lane; the forced marches; and the silvery mist collecting in the hollows of the Blue Ridge Mountains. . . . It's the tawny sea of migrating caribou; those old kerosene lamps (I wish I had a nickel for every one I had to scrub out!); and the enchanting tones of the marimba in the lemon grove on my father's estate. . . . It's the merciless drumming of the jungle rains on the makeshift tin roof; the roar of the crowd when you belt one out of the park; the oranges on Christmas morning; "That Old Gal o' Mine"; and the mournful cry of the loons. . . . It's a wink from old Pops Lundquist as he reaches into his big jar of peppermint sticks; the moans of the dead and dying; and the somehow sad smell of the heliotrope out by the shed. . . . It's the ceaseless droning of a trillion buzzing insects that drives you to the brink of madness; Mom's gingerbread (store-bought never tastes as good, for some reason); and those slick-haired college boys across the hall playing that old 78 of "Muskrat Ramble" every day. . . . Did I mention the sunny smiles of Babs and Jude? Their faces bright as two shiny new pennies? It's all that . . . and more. It's the lonesome wail of the express train to Memphis; the harsh jabbering of a thousand Arabs in the mysteriously fragrant bazaar; cameraman Bill Kenny; and the moon shining coldly down on the stately Matterhorn. . . . It's the pounding on the door in the middle of the night; being pulled from a half-sleep and taken for a ride in the Big Van to interminable hours of beating and torture. . . .

"Let's Get Right to It, Shall We?" A Star Trek Story

by Sandy Frank

"Captain's log, star date 6715.5. We are in orbit around Noldicia, a standard Class M planet, the third in a system of eight. Our mission here is a happy one—to evaluate Noldicia's qualifications for full membership in the Federation. Yet, I am strangely uneasy. Something seems wrong here, though I cannot say what."

"Captain, we are receiving a signal from the surface. It's the council, sir."

"Put it on the screen, Lieutenant Uhura."

"Yes, sir."

Mr. Spock and Dr. McCoy joined Captain Kirk on the bridge as the video picture stabilized. In a large chamber, sitting behind a single, immense desk, were Brenson, the head of the planetary council, and several other council members. All were men, with short hair, and all wore navy blue double-breasted blazers and khaki pants.

"Captain Kirk. It's a pleasure to welcome you to Noldicia. More fun than humans should be allowed to have."

McCoy nudged Kirk and whispered urgently, "That doesn't quite ring true, Jim."

"The pleasure is ours, Councilman Brenson," Kirk replied. "Councilman," he continued, "we are anxious to begin our Federation membership evaluation. I assume you have no objection to our coming down and looking around?"

Before Brenson could answer, he was interrupted by the sound of a Noldician spacecraft passing overhead. "Excuse me, it must have been that awful shrimp salad. Now, where was I? Oh yes, your investigation. We are most eager for you to begin. How many of you will be coming down?"

"Two or three."

"And how much do you weigh?" He went on before Kirk could answer. "Just kidding, Captain. Travel Director Gurtner will see to the arrangements."

The man two seats to Brenson's right spoke up. "That's *Gurnee*. Two e's."

Another council member jumped to his feet. "Run for your lives! It's a trick!"

"No, no. These are only jokes. And just barely, at that." Brenson seemed unperturbed. "In any event, Captain, the sooner we can arrange an appointment for our cable link, the better."

Kirk nodded. The most important benefit of full membership in the Federation was the cable link to the Federation Broadcasting System. Without that link, a planet had to rely on its indigenous television, supplemented in the Noldicians' case by twentieth-century signals just now reaching them from old Earth. Many interplanetary disputes had been quelled by threatening the involved parties with cancellation of FBS programming. "Yes, Councilman, I understand. You will have to find a date when everyone on the planet can be home all day for the cable guy."

"Exactly, Captain. We would like to begin polling our citizens as soon as possible—and I think we all know how painful that can be." Brenson tossed a pencil over his shoulder, breaking the window behind him. "Now, I'm afraid we have other business to attend to.

"Today is Thursday, the day the council members answer their mail. We can speak again tomorrow, which will give these ridiculous haircuts time to grow out." The other council members murmured assent as they ran their hands over their heads in unison. "And if that isn't enough—and, by gosh, don't you think it ought to be—we can arrange for more time next week. Good night, Captain. Drive safely."

Brenson picked up a stack of blue index cards and began to read. "Letter number one. Dear council, What's the deal on the water supply in sector three . . . ."

As the screen went blank, Spock pursed his lips in thought.

The next day, Kirk and Spock prepared to beam down to the surface to look around for themselves. McCoy stayed behind to treat his patients. He had not been happy about staying, protesting, "Dammit, Jim, I'm a doctor," but Kirk had mollified him by pointing out that treating the sick was, indeed, practicing medicine.

As Kirk and Spock entered the transporter, Mr. Scott gave them some advice.

"Ca'n. Be careful whe' y'r do' o' the sur'ace. Ya ne'er no' wha' ca' ha'en i' a situation li' thi'."

Only years of familiarity allowed Kirk to understand. Scotty's speech had become even more garbled lately, his consonants almost completely replaced by glottal stops. McCoy, worried that Scotty might actually strangle one day, had been trying to persuade him to consent to some experimental neurosurgery or at least to moderate his intake of Baruvian brandy, but so far without success.

They toured the surface on Friday. Things seemed normal, if it could be considered normal for people to fill the local parks and auditoriums and spend the day teaching their pets to perform complex but ridiculous stunts. The Noldicians themselves exhibited astonishing coordination, some wearing sticky suits that enabled them to climb up and down the sides of buildings and all dodging with practiced ease the pencils and blue cards that fell to the streets continually from the windows above.

Kirk's vague feeling of unease grew. When they returned to the *Enterprise*, he set Spock to evaluating Noldicia with the ship's scanners and computer.

Spock was waiting for them when they got to the conference room. "Captain, I've run the data we collected through the computer."

"Well, Spock, you must be a very proud young man. So what's the deal with these council weasels? What did the computer have to say?"

"I'm afraid it has not been very helpful, Captain. There is no record of a similar situation anywhere in the galaxy." Spock folded his hands and waited.

McCoy broke in. "Come on, Spock. What the *hell* is going on here?"

Spock looked at him with barely disguised distaste. "As we know from our travels, most planets have societies almost exactly like that of some country on twentieth-century Earth. This one is no exception, but, unfortunately, I have not been able to find the cause of its defects, except that it seems to have some connection to a television show and its host, both long since forgotten."

"Well, no matter what the computer says, we have a decision to make." Kirk got up and began pacing. "The Federation of course wants to embrace all friendly cultures. But can we allow these people to become full Federation members?" He whirled to face his officers. "There's something so odd here. If only I could fully understand it . . . ." He stood frozen in thought for a long moment. He suddenly felt tired, but it was a good kind of tired. Then, smiling at the beautiful simplicity of a sudden insight, he reached out and switched on the intercom to the bridge. "Mr. Sulu, lock in the coordinates of all population centers on Noldicia. And then let's have some fun . . . by destroying stuff—indeed, the entire planet—with a powerful space phaser."

Kirk released the intercom button, cutting off Sulu's whoop of glee. Then as the undetected space-borne parasite that had driven the Noldicians mad set up housekeeping in his own forebrain, he added, to himself, "And I think we all know just how painful that can be."

Treasure Island by Robert Louis Stevenson

by Chris Elliott

"Fifteen men on the dead man's chest—
Yo-ho-ho, and a bottle of rum!"

So sang the bloody pirates of the mighty *Españualo* (their ship). High above in the crisp, morning breeze flies the Skull and Crossed Bones (their flag). "God keep us from a pirate's fury!" They're all here: Long John Silver, Benn Gunn, Capt. Smollett, Barney, and Mack. All carved clearly but delicately through the colorful imagery of Robert Louis Stevenson's marvelously sparkling written word.

The story opens at a tavern or inn (as they were known in turn-of-the-century England), and it is there that Stevenson introduces us to Admiral Benbow. He cuts an ominous figure. Through a series of mishaps, an old, faded treasure map falls into the hands of our hero, Puck. "Find the treasure!" Benbow tells Puck. "Find the treasure, and you shall know all!" And so begins Puck's (and our) adventure.

Puck must unearth the ancient treasure and bring it safely back to Mr. Benbow before a band of bloodthirsty pirates, led by Long John Silver (named for his false arm, which was made of pewter but from a distance looked silver), gets there first.

I found *Treasure Island* enjoyable, to say the least, but also a bit tedious. If you don't keep up with Stevenson's intricate use of language you occasionally find yourself wandering from the text and daydreaming.

Note to the Reader:

OK. I'm sorry! I know I could have put a little more thought into this, but to tell you the truth, the deadline for these essays was today and the publisher put a lot of pressure on the writers to get original material. I just couldn't get it together. I'm really sorry. I've never even read *Treasure Island*. I had to rely on my fellow writers to fill me in on the story.

I'm sure *Treasure Island* is a great piece of literature. If it's anything like Stevenson's other books (*Moby Dick* and *The 39 Steps*), it's got to be terrific!

Late Night Myths

by Gerard Mulligan

Like any institution, *Late Night* has acquired a rich patina of myth and legend over the years. Many viewers, for example, firmly believe that David Letterman was the model for the Gerber baby, or that during one memorable installment of "Stupid Pet Tricks" a cougar taught by its owner to open a pop-top beer can with its teeth ran amok and mauled three audience members and a page before being subdued by an NBC security guard.

When pressed, these viewers will concede that *they* didn't actually see the show in question (a friend of a friend did), but the incident *did* occur, they have no doubt about it. "It's a well-known fact," they say, hurt by your obvious skepticism.

This is an excellent opportunity to sort out some of the myths and realities about the show. It is also an excellent opportunity to remind readers that 55 m.p.h. isn't just a good idea—it's the *law.*

Myth: *Elvis Presley once made a surprise walk-on appearance on the show. He did four songs with the band, chatted amiably with David for a few minutes, then exited to tumultuous applause. Later it was learned that the King of Rock 'n' Roll had actually died in Memphis, Tennessee, three years earlier.*

Fact: Elvis Presley never appeared on *Late Night.* A possible explanation for the story: in the early days of the show, John Chancellor—a frequent guest—was prevailed upon by Dave and the studio audience to do his Elvis impression. He performed "Teddy Bear," "Suspicious Mind," and "Are You Lonesome Tonight?"

Myth: *David's father was a founding member of the singing group the Lettermen.*

Fact: There is no connection between David Letterman and the Lettermen except the mutual respect all entertainers feel for one another.

Myth: *The letters "LNWDL" on the obverse of the Roosevelt dime are some anonymous U.S. Mint employee's tribute to his favorite TV show.*

Fact: There are no such letters on any American coin.

Myth: *The titles on the movie marquees glimpsed briefly in the opening titles for the show are a cryptic salute to a Satanic cult of which David Letterman is New York district chairman.*

Fact: David Letterman does not belong to any Satanic cult in New York.

Myth: *Because of a childhood kindness performed for the young David Letterman, the comedian will never do a joke that insults noted newsman Walter Cronkite, despite the frequent pleas of the show's writers.*

Fact: The newsman in question is Eric Sevareid.

Myth: *"Hal Gurnee"—listed in the show's credits as "Director"—does not exist. It is really just a name owned by NBC, and no more refers to a real person than "Betty Crocker" or "Aunt Jemima" do. As an economy measure, the show has no director, and the listing of "Hal Gurnee" represents a compromise the network worked out with the Director's Guild.*

Fact: Hal Gurnee is a respected director of the kind of television represented by *Late Night*. (Incidentally, similar stories have circulated about Johnny Carson, Merv Griffin, and Diane Sawyer).

Myth: *A very famous movie star once appeared on the show dead drunk and rambled incoherently about his involvement in the Kennedy assassination. The show was never broadcast, and the tape destroyed immediately afterward, on orders of someone at the very highest levels of the U.S. government. Audience members were sworn to secrecy by an obviously shaken Will Lee (the* Late Night *bass player).*

Fact: This legend began circulating shortly after Olivia Newton-John appeared on the show and claimed she had killed Jimmy Hoffa.

Myth: *Larry "Bud" Melman is a fabulously wealthy eccentric who showers money and expensive gifts on David, NBC executives, staff members, and even occasionally audience members. This accounts for his presence on the show.*

Fact: Nothing accounts for his presence on the show.

I hope that this little essay will lay to rest some of the more ludicrous rumors about *Late Night*, but I'm not very optimistic. For one thing, legends are curiously stubborn things to kill. And for another, there are always new ones springing up, like weeds. Lately, for example, the show has been getting letters from all over the country, angrily demanding to know what kind of human being would toss a kitten off a five-story tower just for "kicks."

The Greatest Moments of My Life (I'll Share Them with You)

by Matthew Wickline

Life is a river. Okay, jump in the boat. We're taking a ride down the river of my life. Along the way I'll point out the important sites, special events, tender moments from memory—in effect, everything that isn't obscured by foliage or crudely altered in some way by the Army Corps of Engineers (they're blasting downstream around the mid-70's).

So . . . let's go!

I paid the deposit on the canoe, so I'll steer. You'll be our muscle. Remember—two strokes left, two strokes right, make tiny whirlpools behind your paddle, and *no splashing*. That's it. Oh, you're doing just fine. . . .

Hey, over there on the left bank! That little whippersnapper running and laughing is me at age five! And that featureless kind of rectangular shape rocking back and forth on its rear edge is my dog, Tubulo. I called it a dog for lack of a better name. My father bought Tubulo from an old drifter who came through town every spring with cages full of the things. Well, they were cheaper than real dogs, and that was the important thing to Dad. Sure, without any kind of identifiable appendages or mouth or sensory organs, you can bet the animal needed a lot of care—and for most of its life I sensed that it must have been in a great deal of pain. Still, I loved my little Tubulo, and although I can't be completely sure, I believe he loved me too.

Oh, look over there! See that flimsy sort of half-tepee, half-sugar-cone structure with the big rusty air-conditioning unit hanging off the side? That's the old Injun Cone ice cream stand—my first job. I'm eight years old there and quite proud of my newfound social position. My only complaint is that quarters are already pretty cramped and it's obvious that a continued normal growth rate will put me out of a job within two years. . . . Yeah, that must be my first day. There's my dad walking up and pretending not to notice me. Hear his order?

". . . and if it's not too much trouble, young man, I'll have a *Rum Drunk Halfbreed* with a fudge scalp, and a *Screamin' Squaw Shake* to go."

"Yes, sir!" I fired back with pride. Boy, that was a great day. I remember a few years later, when the Injun Cone burned down. The whole thing went up in a blink—vaporized by a carelessly tossed cigarette. The rumor was that the owner never really owned the property, so as a precautionary measure, he built the stand entirely out of magician's flash paper. . . . It doesn't really matter, I guess—all that remains is a dark circle on the concrete to mark the spot . . . but I have my memories.

What? Yeah, I hear that sound, sure . . . crazy is right . . . like a storm of simultaneously ascending and descending scales, like a thousand untuned flutes caught in the eye of a cyclone—that's my kaleidophone lesson and Mr. DeFioray, my music instructor, is furious with me! Look at me sitting there behind my music stand, trying to endure his angry shouts with my eyes clenched tight. . . . I'm cursing myself for having chosen to learn the most difficult instrument in the modern symphonic orchestra, and, as you know, the only instrument that is also *alive*.

"Oh, Virgin Mary! What must I do to make him understand?! What?!" One thing I'll say for Mr. DeFioray, he worked hard for his stinking two dollars and fifty cents a half hour.

"Please, boy, help an old man and try to understand! You don't *play* a kaleidophone—it's a living thing. You can only learn to *control* its song. . . . *Playing* it only makes it angry. It's angry! I'm angry!"

I'm totally lost. The instrument is fighting me—trying to wriggle free. It's also beginning to sweat and I'm afraid my shirt will be permanently stained. I don't know what to say . . . I want to make my instructor happy but, but . . . out of the confusion, I blurt out my feelings:

"But, Mr. DeFioray, good gosh! Trying to play this thing is . . . well . . . like wrestling with a waterfall . . . uh . . . inside a . . . uh . . . a bag of Styrofoam popcorn stuff . . . know what I mean?"

He stopped. His face was blank a moment—numbed by my stupidity, I thought, then it erupted.

"Yes! Yes! Yes! Oh, Virgin Mary, yes! You *do* understand!" I really felt like I had learned something that day, and Mr. DeFioray, choking back his own sobs of satisfaction as he headed for the door, told me to keep the two-fifty. Real shame, though . . . there he is, moments later driving his hydro-bus into the massive whirling blades of Swane County Wind Dam. . . . He never had a chance.

Hey, that's my marching band knee deep in alluvial mud over there!

By *my* I mean *my personal* marching band. I didn't like our high school band (no one did) so I started my own. I called it Pep Incorporated, and within weeks of its formation we were asked to replace the school band for all regular-season football games. Eventually the school band, or Marching Crests, was dissolved. A lot of those guys are still bitter about the whole thing. They say I'm vicious, that there's a lump of obsidian where my heart should be. But the fact of the matter is: they stank. This is America and I paid for my college up front and in cash with the proceeds . . . so . . . too bad!

Boy, this river is moving awful fast. We're starting to miss some things —like just back there was another great moment. I'm opening the letter accepting me to the Chance Institute, where I would eventually learn Randomography and the Happensciences . . . right there under those hanging vines I'm gluing old radio and TV parts to my first college girlfriend. That's a pretty complicated story, and we're already pretty far downriver . . . oh, we're missing so much. Look up there, already I'm signing my contract with *Late Night* and subsequently tithing away 10 percent of my savings and all my personal effects to the show. . . . Gosh, so much I'd love to tell you about, but that familiar floating barrier just ahead means we've arrived all too soon at the present. There are the NOW Rangers approaching on the River Authority Barge. They'll want to see your papers . . . don't worry, it's very informal . . . just a routine precaution.

Well, sorry we couldn't see more, but the river's much faster than I expected. I can't help it—it's this life—it's this TV business. Everything's fast. One minute you're looking around on the ground for a piece of rope to hold your pants up, the next minute somebody's handing you a trophy and shoving your photograph on the cover of *People* magazine. The next minute you're president of the network and you have a sneaking suspicion that by tomorrow morning you might be dead drunk at the bottom of a dipsey dumpster and starting the whole thing all over again. Still, I think I've learned a couple of things from this old river. First, that there are no words for the things I truly love—but that every time I've tried to make up those words and use them in my daily speech, I've been called an ass. And the second thing is that life's greatest moments aren't worth living, unless they can be shared with someone like you . . . unless you turn out to be an inmate at a maximum security prison with a history of violent crimes or something like that (there's really no way for me to know). But, whoever you are, the important thing, the *most* important thing, is that you paddle pretty well. And to me . . . on this river . . . that's all that really matters.

A Reply to Our Critics

by Randy Cohen

When *Late Night* began, everyone involved was determined to make it just a little different from other shows—in the guests we booked, the comedy we wrote, and the products that bore our name. This is not to deny the possibility of an occasional slip-up. A zipper might jam on a *Late Night* tote; I don't say it couldn't happen. I do say that no one would intentionally make sausages out of "reptiles, amphibians, and traces of a human spleen," as the USDA laboratory analysis inexplicably concludes. However, to eliminate any ambiguity, when we say that Dave's Country Sausage is made "with his mom's own Indiana recipe," obviously we don't mean Dave's actual mom; we mean his TV mom. The recipe comes from the actress who plays his mom on every pack—Miss Helen Hayes, the first lady of America's breakfast-meat industry, who throughout a distinguished career has used only the finest natural ingredients. As for her claim to being "shocked and humiliated" to find herself on the wrapper, frankly, I'm baffled. In any case, while I can't speak for the show's other writers, it was always my intention to donate my sausage royalties to the United Fund.

Certain so-called consumer advocates have pointed the finger at the *Late Night* Yard and Garden Centers, with their familiar neon caricatures of Dave and Paul—"The Yard Boys"—on those big signs all along the Interstate. I'm the first to admit that few customers would deliberately buy a lawnmower that bursts into flames ninety seconds after you start it up. But we've done everything we could to put things right—made repairs where practical, granted nearly full refunds, and stopped buying mowers through Mr. Ngurda, our purchasing agent in . . . well, I believe Mr. Ngurda had multinational sources. These days, however, we buy only from famous-name suppliers. Now, I don't know what the power-mower policy is at the *Today Show,* but here at *Late Night* we make this pledge: when a mower ignites, our logo comes right off.

Given this commitment to excellence, surely we're the last people you'd expect to " . . . cause permanent, disfiguring injuries through overweening greed and a total indifference to safety," as one World Court judge phrased it. Naturally, we regret any loss of life associated with our *Late Night* Structural Steel, but is this particular catastrophe really the fault of Dave's unique Bessemer process? Might it not be blamed on what strikes me as a whimsical design for a railroad bridge, particularly for a tropical region? Couldn't it be attributed to the slap-dash methods of the native work crew? Surely justice demands that we wait for the report of the investigating engineer after he's examined all the evidence. (And by *all,* I include certain lurid magazines found near the quarters of Mr. Ngurda, the foreman and a fellow of dubious ethics, with whom we no longer have any dealings.) That is, if we can expect such niceties as due process in a part of the world so riven by tribal loyalties and religious mania.

Despite these mishaps, I hope our efforts are not unappreciated. Our job is to produce a lively television show; we didn't *have* to operate a Caribbean-chartered bank. I concede that the precipitous collapse of Banco de Noche Tarde caught many of our small depositors by surprise. But look: the money is gone, and all of the congressional hearings in the world won't bring it back. So why don't you quit your damn bellyaching!

I wish I could be in New York to elaborate on these matters, but, sadly, the other writers and I are kept occupied here in Costa Rica. As you might imagine, it is a cumbersome business phoning the comedy into the show each day. But rest assured, as soon as our lawyers give us the OK to return, we'll be back, bringing along more of the innovative comedy you've come to expect and plenty of great ideas for new *Late Night* products.

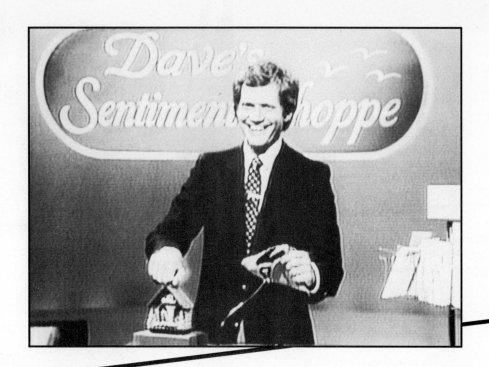

Dave's Sentiment Shoppe

Like most people, over the years I've been approached about investing in a number of business ventures. Some looked promising —for instance, last fall I almost went into a distributorship for a company called Amway. But I never found anything that suited my personality until just recently. In the not too distant future, we'll be opening over 600 Dave's Sentiment Shoppes across the country. I hope they'll be your one-stop center for sharing and caring supplies. So I thought I'd use this section of the book to present some sample merchandise.

Naturally, Dave's Sentiment Shoppes stock the usual holiday and birthday cards, but we also carry a number of specialty cards to cover the entire spectrum of human emotions. For example, our **obsession cards.**

Strawberry Shortcake Shrunken Head

This adorable gift is just as much at home on your mantel or knickknack shelf as it is dangling from the rearview mirror of the family sedan. It's the **Strawberry Shortcake shrunken head**—your favorite merchandising character in a fun new novelty format.

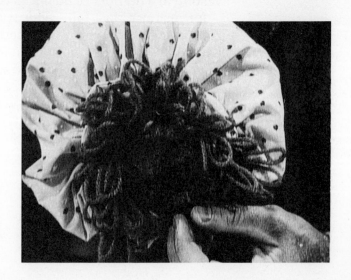

You've Always Been A Winner, SON

At least you were, before you decided to throw your God-given talent away.

And our **disappointment card.**

Kid's Pencil Case

It's never too early to teach youngsters just how short their time on earth is. Now they can learn this valuable lesson along with readin', writin', and 'rithmetic as they use this beautiful **velvet-lined-coffin pencil case.** A subtle reminder to Junior that his days are numbered.

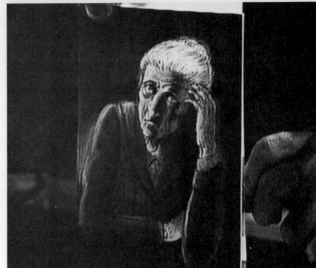

Because your friend's ailment is minor doesn't mean you shouldn't spend a dollar on a card.

Collector Vermin Thimbles

Everybody knows the problem with collecting those prized commemorative thimbles: the figures reproduced on them are just too small. That's not the case with this new series of **collector thimbles.** Each features a life-sized, hand-painted illustration of a bothersome insect. Here's a stag beetle, a boll weevil, and a chigger—they look real enough to give you a nasty bite or rash!

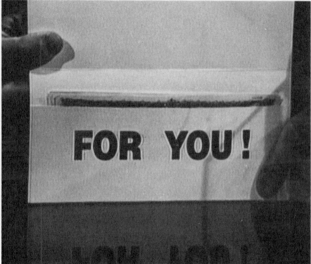

If you are a defense contractor or a Washington lobbyist, cash is often the very best gift you can give. Here's a gracious way to present it.

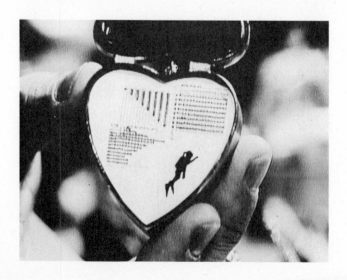

Everyone's seen those miniature lockets that open up to reveal a wedding date or an "I love you." Here's a more practical locket made of solid gold containing a tiny but complete **Coast Guard decompression table.** Every day it tells your mate, "Honey, I don't ever want you to get the bends."

And finally, sometimes you just have to let a card say what's in your heart for you.

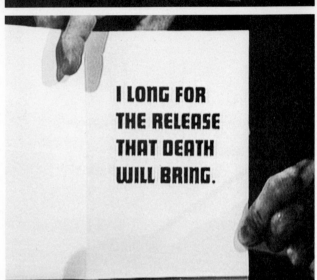

I've always enjoyed those clever little slogans you see printed on **coffee mugs.** For some reason, they never fail to give me a chuckle. Here's one that'll brighten up any office.

When you're looking for a gift for an elderly aunt or grandmother, you can't go wrong with adorable little ceramic figurines. Here's a handcrafted set of figures depicting **a road crew on lunch break.**

Key chains worn on the belt used to be popular items until they became a symbol of gay pride. Now straight folks can wear them again, with this **brass key ring** that tells the world "I'm not that way."

We're Letting You Go

It's never a very festive occasion when someone has to be fired from his job—that is, unless you break the news to him with this **whimsical party banner.** Just hang it across his doorway, and go out for pancakes.

Loser Cards

Greeting cards have always been available for the new bride or the recent college grad. But until now there's never been a line of cards for people who leech off their friends and refuse to work. These new **loser cards** are perfect for anyone who's living on someone else's couch. For example:

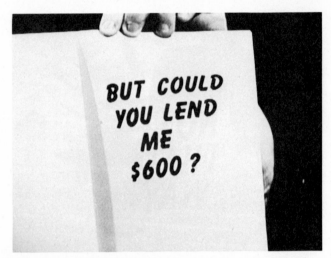

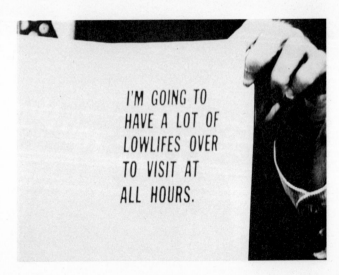

Funny Ape Poster

For those days when everything seems to go wrong, there's nothing like a funny animal poster to put things in the proper perspective. Here's a wise old gorilla who seems to have the right attitude. The caption reads, "You think you have problems—my skin is crawling with parasites."

You know, elderly folks often have to monitor their blood pressure at home but blood pressure gauges are always covered with confusing numbers. For folks who just want to know if they're sick or well, how about this **adorable Black Forest blood pressure cottage**? If the pale fräulein appears, all's well. But if the red-faced burgermeister comes out, call the doctor.

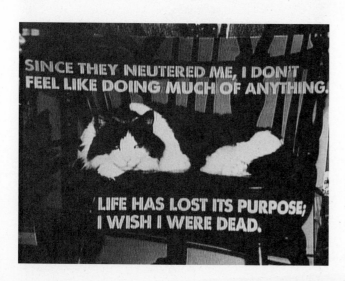

Cat Poster

Is there anybody who doesn't love a **cute cat poster**? Well, if there is, I haven't met him. And this poster adds a delightful note of realism to the usual whimsy that makes these products such heavy profit items.

We've all seen **decorative covers** designed to conceal ugly electric stove burners.

They're great, but where do you put them while you're cooking? No problem, with these **burner cover caddys. . . .**

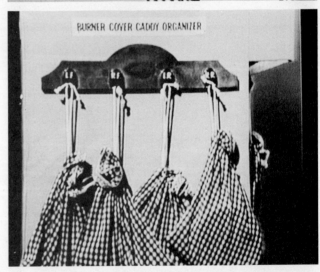

But with four of these things to deal with, they can get in the way. . . . Unless you have this **burner cover caddy organizer. . . .**

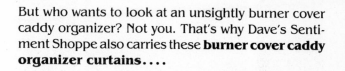

But who wants to look at an unsightly burner cover caddy organizer? Not you. That's why Dave's Sentiment Shoppe also carries these **burner cover caddy organizer curtains....**

But plain old curtains can be so drab. They just cry out for felt appliqués to liven them up. Of course it would be a shame to let kitchen grease ruin these lovely appliquéd curtains. That's why you should protect them with this sturdy **splatter guard kitchen partition ....**

Now I know you're saying to yourself, "Gee, it's going to be a lot of trouble moving that partition around for mopping the floor."... Not with the **burner cover caddy organizer curtain splatter screen partition winch lifter.**

Psycho Cards

Everybody loves *somebody* sometime . . . even dangerous sociopaths and deranged criminals. That's why this shop offers a variety of greeting cards to and for psychos . . . . Here's a couple of nice ones.

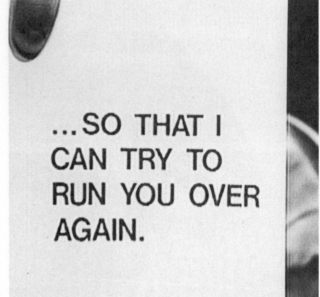

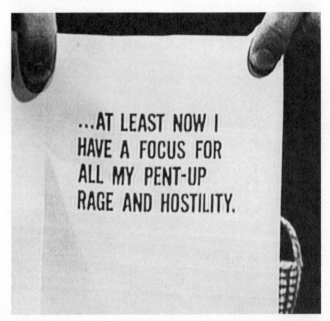

Here are two cards to send when you're having trouble coming to terms with a business associate.

Taxi Etiquette

Anyone who spends any amount of time in New York City is going to have at least one occasion to use a taxi cab. Even if you never leave the hotel, it's just the kind of thing you end up doing in New York City. As with all things, your experience will be much more tolerable if you bother to learn and use the rules of etiquette.

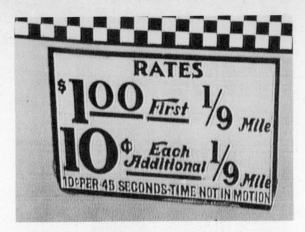

You'll notice that the cab fare is posted right on the door: $1.00 for the first 1/9 of a mile, and then 10¢ for each additional mile.

That's why you have to remember to bring along plenty of dimes. It's correct form to pay 1/9 of a mile at a time.

Once inside the cab, the first thing to do is get to know your host.

Every New York cabdriver is considerate enough to place a photo of himself on the dashboard.

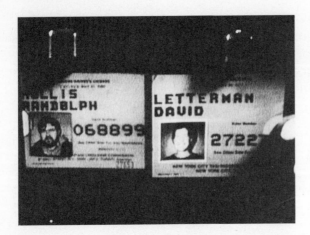

As a passenger, you should be just as considerate.
   Bring along a photo I.D. of your own to place right next to his.

Your next task is to check out the equipment and make sure that everything is in good working order. Take the radio mike off its hook and announce "Attention, K-Mart shoppers. Everything on aisle six is now thirty percent off." This helps to establish rapport with your driver. Every New York City cabbie surely loves plenty of high jinks.

Think of the cab as your home away from home. You're renting the space, so you might as well make yourself comfortable.

That's why I like to bring along certain items that make me feel more at home.

For example, these little Hawaiian dolls. They make me feel like I'm right in my living room. Incidentally,

New York City cabbies actually prefer them to tips. So it's a good idea to bring a big sackful.

And I have yet to ride in a cab that doesn't cry out for curtains!!

Along about ⅝ of a mile is a good time to have a little fun. Your cabdriver works long hard hours and there's nothing he likes more than fun-filled surprises.

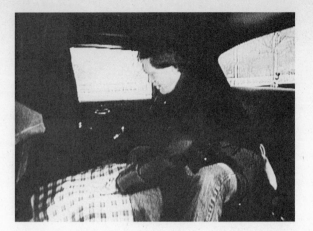

"Hey, Mr. Driver. Can you take me to Yankee Stadium?"

Surprisingly, not everyone realizes that a New York City cab is a perfect location for a romantic dinner. The jump seat makes a nice little table. However, it's a good idea to bring along your own tablecloth, unless you don't mind the idea of eating on wads of hardening gum.

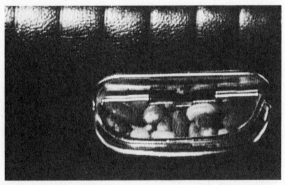

A few dining hints: the change containers make ideal mint and nut cups.

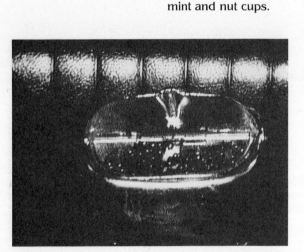

And if there's a sight that whets the appetite more than an ashtray full of caviar, I have yet to see it.

Now, sit back and enjoy a soothing cocktail. Believe me, *nothing* enhances the palate and bouquet of a fine imported wine like the aroma of exhaust fumes.

Finally, all that you really need to make the evening perfect is some romantic music. A radio or tape deck will suffice. But for me, nothing beats the thrill of live music.

All set to go, Uncle Pete?

The Late Night Bookmobile

Everyone knows that *Late Night* has a commitment to producing top-quality television entertainment. But not everyone knows that there's a much smaller and less enthusiastic commitment to producing fine works of literature. Well, it's true. We're also doing all we can to encourage the good habit of reading.

So open the garage doors of your imagination, and let's take a spin on the blacktop highway of good reading.

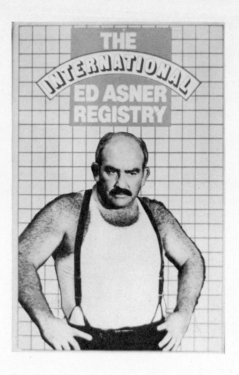

A few years back, for a price, *The International Star Registry* let you name a star for a friend. Well, here's a delightful variation on that idea. It's **The International Ed Asner Registry.** For just twenty-five dollars you can name a hair on Ed Asner's back for one of your friends or loved ones. . . . There's no better way to say, "I think you're special."

After books about fairies, gnomes, and elves came out a few years back, you might have said to yourself, "What's next." Well, we've got it right here. Now you can take an imaginary journey through the magical and enchanted kingdom of **Ticks.**

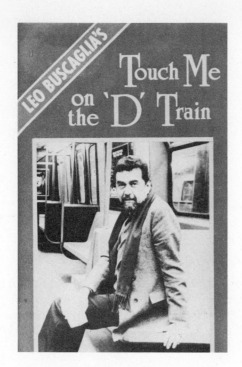

This man has been called the love professor and the founder of hug therapy. Fans will welcome his new book on New York City. It's *Leo Buscaglia's Touch Me on the 'D' Train.*

Money-saving travel books have long been a staple of the best-seller list: *Europe on $5 a Day, France on $15 a Day.* . . . And now we have this new volume —Stacy Keach's *England on No Dollars a Day.*

The correspondence of famous people often makes for great books, and this one is no exception. It's the complete set of letters from John Chancellor to the late Princess Grace, and it's called *So What Is It, I'm Not Good Enough for You?*

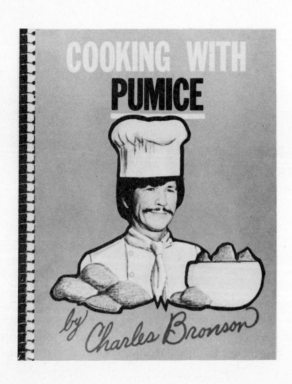

A new cookbook by a man who's as at home in the kitchen as he is wasting creeps . . . *Cooking with Pumice* by Charles Bronson.

Former President Gerald Ford has directed his knowledge of government to the writing of serious science fiction. In the hopes of warning us about what the future may hold, here's his first sci-fi novel: **When Potato Bugs Rule!**

And finally, here's a coffeetable book that would make a splendid gift: *Larry! A Celebration.* Perhaps the most lavishly illustrated tribute to guys named Larry ever published in the West. Olivier, Hovis, Byrd, Storch, Hagman, Melman . . . they're all here.

NAME YOUR BABY WHEN YOU'RE ANGRY

There are a lot of helpful books for parents-to-be, including collections of names for newborns. Here's one that takes a different approach: ***Name Your Baby When You're Angry.*** Some of the suggestions: Crib Lizard, Wobbly, Mr. Drips, Gurgle Jerk, Thimble Nose, Drool Bunny, Stroller Snake, Scumbo, Rat Bag, Slug, Bonehead, Loser, Wormy, Stump, Gas Bag, Weasel.

THE WORLD'S DAMNDEST TYPOS

Can't get enough of those bleeps, bloops, and blunders? Well, now the publishing industry has gotten into the act with this collection, ***The World's Damndest Typos.*** Hundreds of best-loved authors are caught in the act of being themselves as they turn "Tuesday" into "Tubsday," "New York" into "New Pork," and mistakenly state that Gandhi was the spiritual leader of "Indiana."

Here's a book that lets kids get to know their favorite stars better while using their sense of touch: *A Child's Book of Celebrity Textures.*

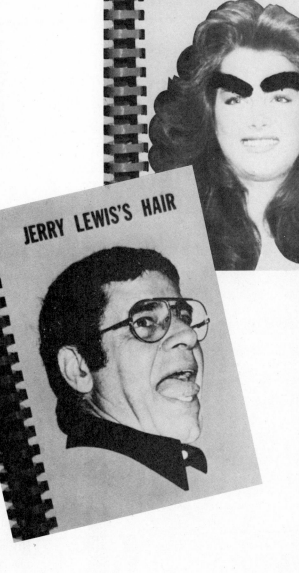

And finally, here's something that can teach the kids about the unexpected twists on the road of life. It's called **The Muppets All Die and Go to Hell.** Yes, sometimes it doesn't seem fair, does it?

Here's a question we hear all the time: Is there life on other planets? If there is, who's to say it's not *lowlife*? That's the premise of this new Isaac Asimov saga: **Mars Needs a Shave and a Hot Meal.**

TV's Victoria Principal has had a lot of success with her books *The Body Principal* and *The Beauty Principal*. This one's sure to be a best-seller too: ***The Industrial Machine Principle***—lots of tips on operating hydraulic jacks, forklifts, and dredgers.

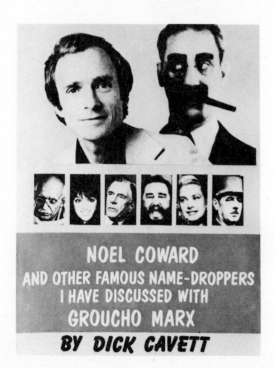

Dick Cavett has finally given in to the clamor for more stories about himself and famous celebrities in . . . ***Noel Coward and Other Famous Name-Droppers I Have Discussed with Groucho Marx.***

Here's a children's book from the people who publish Golden Books. It's called **Beaks—The Big Nose Book.** Here's actor Karl Malden . . . TV's Judd Hirsch . . . former football great Joe Namath . . . ex-Beatle Ringo Starr . . . newsman Marvin Kalb.

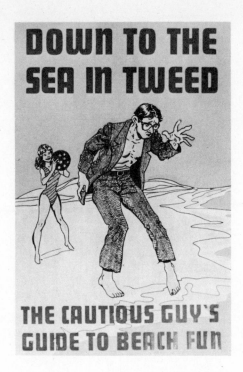

Here's some good summer reading . . . ***Down to the Sea in Tweed: The Cautious Guy's Guide to Beach Fun.***

Following the success of Shirley MacLaine's best-selling *Out on a Limb*, in which she discusses her experiences in an earlier life, comes a new publication: ***"There Are Tiny People in My Salt Shaker."***

Here's a guide for those awkward moments right after you've started to rob someone: **What Do You Say After You Say Hands Up!**

Actor/playwright Sam Shepard has always drawn on his personal experiences in his plays, and his latest one is certainly no exception: ***Boy oh Boy, I'm Actually Sleeping with Jessica Lange.***

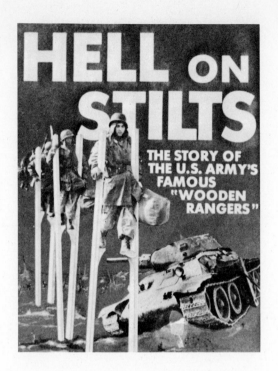

Here's a book that's selling well this summer, a favorite among history buffs: ***Hell on Stilts: The Story of the U.S. Army's Famous "Wooden Rangers,"*** the high-walking regiment that broke the back of Hitler's war machine. As a matter of fact, they were said to have been at Anzio.

For those pre-teens who are a little apprehensive about becoming young adults and starting to smoke, the tobacco institute has published ***A Child's First Book of Smoking.***

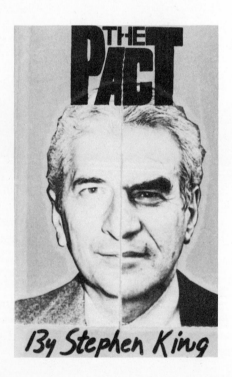

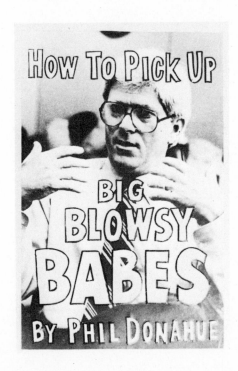

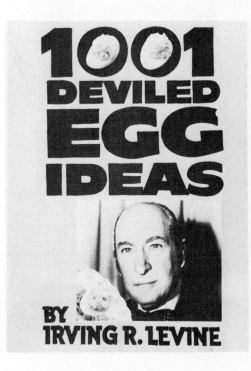

Spring Quiz

Each year, spring comes as a welcome relief—putting an end to long months spent cooped up indoors, sitting in front of the TV. Now at last it's time to carry the set out back to the patio, where you can stretch out on the lounge chair. And to help you through this tough transition period, we've prepared a spring quiz.

For most people, spring begins:

A. on March 21
B. when the baseball season opens
C. when a new von Bülow trial is announced

San Diego Padres first baseman Steve Garvey has:

A. the durability of Gehrig
B. the consistency of DiMaggio
C. the forearms of Popeye

The young fans who pour into Yankee Stadium to root for their heroes are known as:

A. Yankee juniors
B. Yankee boosters
C. parole violators

This time of year, street fairs are a great place to pick up:

A. shirts from the fifties
B. jackets from the sixties
C. body lice from total strangers

For all his contributions to the game, Joe Garagiola will be assigned:

A. to be America's goodwill ambassador worldwide
B. a place in the Hall of Fame
C. his own special level of hell

Elevator Etiquette

When you live or work in New York City, there is one thing you can be sure of: you are going to have to spend a lot of time riding in elevators. But as with any form of travel, your ride will be a lot more pleasant if you learn the rules of elevator etiquette.

Fourteenth floor is a fine floor. Hi. I'm Tom Gammil. Second floor.

If there are already people on board, it is customary to introduce yourself to each of them by name and floor destination. For example: "Hello, I'm Dave Letterman. Fourteenth floor."

Second floor. What a wimp! Couldn't you walk up *one* flight of stairs?

This is an example of an elevator faux pas. Never deride a fellow passenger based on his or her floor selection.

If no one else has already done so, feel free to appoint yourself elevator captain. Your first duty is to

check the equipment: be sure to push every button in the car. And don't forget to test the safety alarm.

Every elevator car comes equipped with a standard electrical outlet. Why? For your personal use! So take advantage of the time to do some sanding or touch up your appearance.

Now then, remember that every elevator has a posted weight capacity. It is your responsibility to make sure that the weight total in the elevator doesn't exceed this limit. That's why it's important to always carry a pocket calculator. When a new passenger boards who

threatens the weight-capacity total, it is your duty to ask him to leave. Tell him simply, "Sorry, tubby. Get another car." It's for his own safety, and he will thank you for it.

Lastly, in the event of elevator music, is it proper to ask someone to dance? You bet. But be considerate. Take into account floor destination.

The elevator is a wonderful way to make new friends, and isn't that what traveling is all about?

Dog Poetry

Dave's Arts and Crafts

Anyone who knows me knows I like nothing better than spending endless hours in my workshop making lovely gifts for my family and friends. I'd like to share some of my favorite workshop projects with you in a section of the book I've arbitrarily entitled "Dave's Arts and Crafts."

Tobacco Play Hair

Moms know that kids love to play "grown-up," so I came up with a fun, wholesome way to do just that. All they need are a pack of cigarettes and a jar of rubber cement to have hours of fun with **loose tobacco play hair**—now any kid can have a full beard or hairy chest in just minutes.

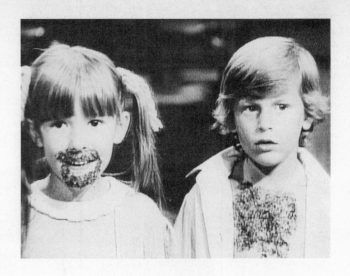

Movie-Novel Thongs

Paperback novelizations of hit motion pictures always pile up at the end of the summer. But why throw them out when you can make them into attractive **beach or shower thongs**? Just attach some nonallergenic Neoprene strips to the covers, and you're in business.

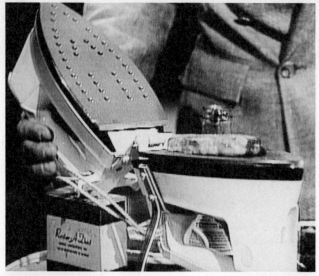

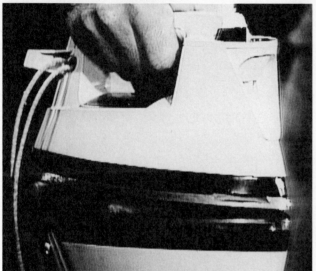

Household Steaker

When you want a quick steak sandwich but don't want to gunk up a lot of pans, what do you do? Well, you can do what I did. All you need is a hinge, some epoxy, and a couple of steam irons, and you can make this: the **Household Steaker**! You almost forget the certain danger of electrical fire when you hear that appetizing sizzle.

Lloyd Bridges Denture-Holder

I think we all know there's no more unappealing sight than dentures floating free in a glass of water. But with a little work and some imagination, you can dress up your night table with this eye-catching container and put a smile on the face of *Sea Hunt* star Lloyd Bridges.

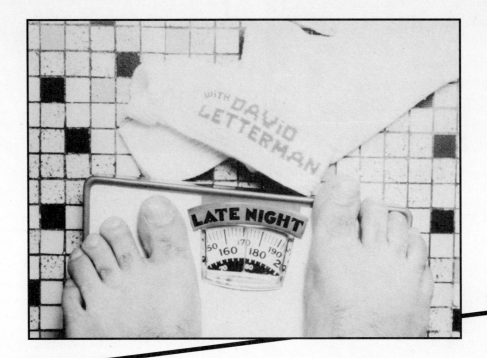

Laundry Etiquette

Recently it has come to my attention that a lot of our viewers do not know how to behave properly at a Laundromat and subsequently have been letting their hygiene go all to hell. So for their benefit, and ours, we tackle the sensitive topic of Laundromat etiquette.

A Laundromat is a public place. When you walk in, it is customary to introduce yourself to everyone by name and stubborn washday problem.

This breaks the ice and provides a handy conversation starter.

Next, you are faced with the arduous task of selecting just the right machine for your needs. Like, for instance, the first one was busy, and the one next to that is full of minnows. And I can see by Machine #3 that it's time for our next rule.

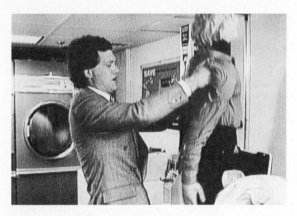

You'll find that every Laundromat has at least one machine which is partially full of water that refuses to drain. This by no means renders it useless. What do you do?

That's why no trip to the Laundromat is complete without some powdered soup mix, tender new potatoes, fresh or frozen vegetables, and a nice corned beef. . . . Turn the setting to hot, and in only minutes, you'll have a hearty New England boiled dinner that the whole Laundromat can enjoy. Be sure to bring along plenty. Nothing makes folks work up an appetite like the atmosphere of a Laundromat.

The old washday saw still holds true today. Rule #2: *Always take your clothes off before you do your laundry.*

Be sure you do not try to wash your clothes while you are still in them.

Here's something that's fun to do. Try to guess what a person is like by looking at his laundry when he's not around.

For instance, this is a big guy but he's obviously kind of a wimp.

Which brings us to Rule #3: Leave other people's laundry alone.

Once the machine begins its cycle, you have about twenty minutes to kill. What do you do now? I suggest you be creative—the possibilities for having fun are limitless! OK, the possibilities aren't *limitless*, but there are a couple of things you can do.

For instance, if you clean out all the dryer filters, you can make a lint man! Really pathetic kids seem to like them just fine.

Or bring along a water pistol full of ink! No one really cares if they get unsightly stains because what the heck! *They're already at the Laundromat!!*

But my favorite way to pass the time is to install one of these hypno-disks in any empty dryer. More than good clean entertainment, the fringe benefits are fantastic. Once you have convinced any fellow patrons to watch for only five minutes, you will be able to have them under your complete control for hours at a time. Now send them out for a pizza and an eight-pack, and your washday problems will *really* start to brighten.

Viewer Mail

Once a week on *Late Night*, we answer our viewer mail on the show. We are often accused of writing these letters ourselves, but we don't (we don't write anything ourselves unless we have to).

No—these are letters from actual folks; members of our vast North American viewing audience who have a burning desire to be heard and at least 22 cents in loose change.

And so, to these time-wasting freeloaders, we dedicate the following section.

Oct 15/83

Dear David,

I have this <u>very</u> important problem that I'm begging for your assistance with. I've been a loyal fan of "Late Night" since the late 1950's (this is <u>not</u> the prevailing problem though) and I've usually enjoyed your show in the serene quiet of my family room. Unfortunately, this year I've moved into a house with four <u>very</u> VOCIFEROUS housemates (and numerous other "sixth" members of our household).

The dilemma is as follows: the most inconvienient time that my friends choose to hold their "raise the roof" sessions is at exactly 12:30 AM when I just sit down to watch your monolouge. In they trudge!!! and they inebriated (after many hours of hand to glass combat at the pub) decide to revalate at an ear-piercing decibal level, that evenings goings on.

Yes, David, I have to resort to lip reading which becomes MOST tiresome after awhile!!! My favour I <u>implore</u> of you is, for the first twenty minutes of your show each night, could you speak VERY LOUDLY and ENUNCIATE just a bit more an if I perchance have to resort to lip-reading (for when a crowd of six or more of my friends get together and drown out a sonic boom) I can do so with greater ease. Or, how about close captioning?????????

Thanks for hearing me out Dave! I'm sure you can find it in your heart to provide a solution to my dilemma (opening up my machine gun on the whole lot of them won't work either)

Trying (desperately) to hang onto every word you say,

Meriann Z▓▓▓▓
Kingston ONT, CANADA

Meriann: Because of the technical nature of your question, we're going to turn to our very own Jimmy Fitzgerald in his "Technician's Corner."

From the way you've described your problem, Meriann, I think you're wrong—opening up on them with a machine gun *would* solve the problem.

To be more precise, since the element of surprise is important in this kind of operation, you'll want to burst in on them with a submachine gun.

The .45 caliber Thompson M-1928 is the best submachine gun in existence. It certainly has the room-clearing firepower you need to deal with your thoughtless friends. But if the weight of the tommy gun bothers you . . .

. . . then you might try a 9-millimeter weapon, like this classic MP-40.

As the old saying goes, Meriann, "When in doubt, shoot it out." But remember, safety first.

I SUPPOSE THAT YOU THINK OF YOURSELF & OTHER ENTERTAINERS AS BEING _IMPORTANT_! HAH! LET ME PUT IT IN PERSPECTIVE FOR YOU, DAVE:

YOU ARE ONE OF 10,000 BILLION LIVING ORGANISMS THAT HAVE INHABITED THIS PLANET SINCE THE CREATION OF LIFE ITSELF. THE PLANET THAT YOU LIVE ON IS A SMALL, ORDINARY, ROCK SPHERE ORBITING A COMMON LITTLE SUN; TUCKED AWAY IN AN OBSCURE CORNER OF A PLAIN OLD SPIRAL GALAXY. ASSUMING THAT YOU WEIGH 1000 lbs., YOUR MASS WOULD BE ONE BILLION BILLION BILLION BILLIONTH OF THE TOTAL MASS OF THE KNOWN UNIVERSE. IMPORTANT? NOT HARDLY!

SIGNED,
JOHN C.
LANSDALE, PA

John: Your perspective is very interesting, but I think you fail to perceive the full scope of this very complicated subject—perhaps this section of the award-winning science film entitled *The Universe and You,* produced by Bell Laboratories in cooperation with the Smithsonian Institution and the National Aeronautics and Space Administration, will help clear things up. . . .

Corrected Pages 194–197 to Be Inserted in Badly Bungled First Printing

> I SUPPOSE THAT YOU THINK OF YOURSELF & OTHER ENTERTAINERS AS BEING _IMPORTANT_! HAH! LET ME PUT IT IN PERSPECTIVE FOR YOU, DAVE:
>
> YOU ARE ONE OF 10,000 BILLION LIVING ORGANISMS THAT HAVE INHABITED THIS PLANET SINCE THE CREATION OF LIFE ITSELF. THE PLANET THAT YOU LIVE ON IS A SMALL, ORDINARY, ROCK SPHERE ORBITING A COMMON LITTLE SUN; TUCKED AWAY IN AN OBSCURE CORNER OF A PLAIN OLD SPIRAL GALAXY. ASSUMING. THAT YOU WEIGH 1000 lbs., YOUR MASS WOULD BE ONE BILLION BILLION BILLION BILLIONTH OF THE TOTAL MASS OF THE KNOWN UNIVERSE. IMPORTANT? NOT HARDLY!
>
> SIGNED,
> JOHN C.
> LANSDALE, PA

John, your perspective is very interesting, but I think you fail to perceive the full scope of this very complicated subject—perhaps this section of the award-winning science film entitled *The Universe and You,* produced by Bell Laboratories in cooperation with the Smithsonian Institution and the National Aeronautics and Space Administration, will help clear things up...

NARRATOR:
... your mass would be one billion, billion, billion, billionth the total mass of the known universe...

Let's go a step further...

and look at a contrast, not of size...

...but of significance...

For example...

...entertainer David Letterman has an average viewing audience of well over six million people.

He makes use of the National Broadcasting Company...

...which has over five hundred thousand employees...

...across the United States...

...and abroad...

...and his salary, although not yet known, is believed to be such...

...that he could quit his job right now and be a wealthy man for a hundred years.

By contrast, John C. of Lansdale, Pennsylvania, has...

. . . *no job* . . .

. . . *no friends* . . .

. . . and interviews with his parents suggest that he soon will have *no home*.

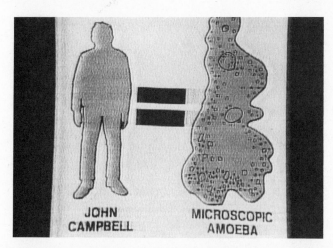

Yes, John C. might as well be an amoeba . . .

. . . to such a man,
    as David Letterman!

fin.

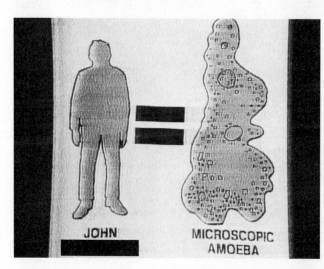

Blue Hill, Me 07614
Oct 27th

Dear Mr. Letterman,

How come we never see it raining or snowing outside your window. I can hardly believe that it never rains or snows in New York City And How come we never hear police or fire alarm sirens. The last time I was in New York City, I couldn't get one wink of sleep on account of the noise on the streets. But there is no noise coming from outside, your window How come?

Larry W▮▮▮▮▮▮

Larry: You were probably in New York a couple of years ago—about the time when there was all that construction noise when they were building the giant climate-dome. . . . Well, the mammoth plastic-and-steel bubble has been in place for quite a while now—and every day here in New York City it's a balmy 68 degrees. No rain, no snow.

Dear Dave,
Since the first time I had seen your show this past summer I have become ~~addicted~~ ~~to Late Night~~. When school started this year I found It harder and harder to gain full consciousness in the mourning after watching Late Night the night before. I solved this problem with a simple and obvious solution, I dropped out of Highschool in my third year. Since I have made this great sacrafise for you Dave, I was wondering If you could put on an educational segment in Late Night so I don't fall back in my education.

Thanks Dave,
A Devoted Fan
Dan T~~~~~~

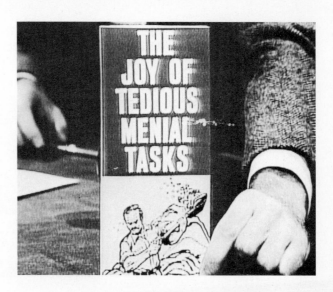

Dan: We certainly do appreciate your dropping out of high school, but we don't really have any educational segments planned for the time being. However, in the meantime, we'll be sending you this pamphlet to help you prepare for the future—"The Joy of Tedious Menial Tasks."

Well Dave,

You finally made It. You really hit the Bigtime with this one. It took Terry Bradshaw almost 10 years of football and a tonge, and even Bullwinkle hasn't reached this Plateau of human achievement. Gosh we've all impressed down here—

Anxiously Awaiting your Next amazing Feat,

Scott P.

Is there a wide screen version coming out soon?

Scott: When I was starting out, I did some modeling work. Here's some of the appliances I modeled for:

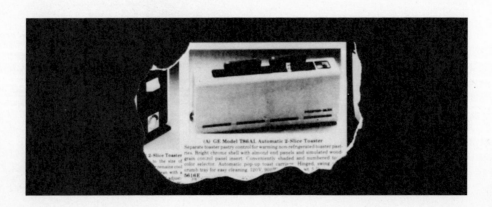

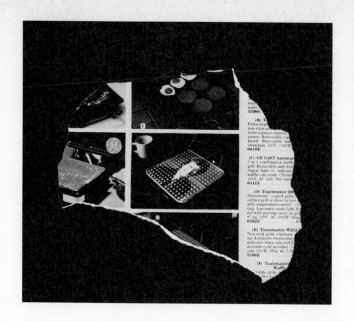

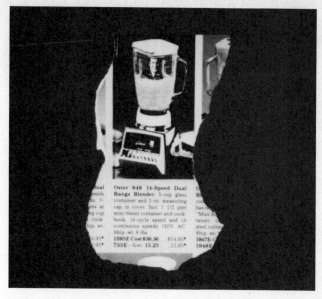

Talk Show Etiquette

Booking guests on a show such as *Late Night* is a difficult and time-consuming task. Sooner or later, just about everyone will be called upon to be a talk show guest. In the event that you do become a guest on our show, your interview will be a lot more pleasant if you take the time to learn the accepted rules of talk show etiquette.

Rule #1: No beach attire. No shirt, no shoes—no interview.

This guest has made a very basic talk show faux pas. Which leads us to Rule #2: Know who and where your host is.

Every guest receives a photo of the host . . .

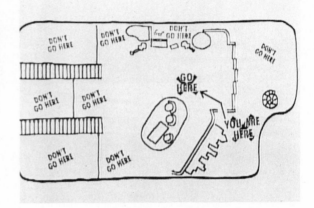

. . . and a map of where to find him. If you get lost, use them.

Rule #3: Take off your Walkman.

If you're booked as a guest on this show, at least *pretend* to be interested.

When you walk onto the set, the host will shake your hand.

It is customary to take advantage of this opportunity to slip the host a hundred. He will like you better and ask nicer questions.

Hello, Marge? Put the doggie on the phone.

Hello, Ginger? How's the little doggie?

Rule #4: Even if they assure you that they'll just watch quietly and won't be any trouble, *don't bring your parents.* Sorry, but it's our show policy.

Rule #5: The phone is here for *my* use only. No personal calls during the show.

What do you mean, "Come back any time"? I've only been here eight minutes!

Rule #6: When your interview is over, just go quietly. When I say, "Thank you very much. Come back any time," what I mean is, take a hike.

Lastly, if you're booked as a guest, try not to die on the show.

A dead guest is a dull guest. It puts a damper on the proceedings. And there might be a comedian following you.

The Writers

From left to right, front row: Larry Jacobson, Steve O'Donnell, David Letterman, Fred Graver. *Middle row:* Jeff Martin, Sandy Frank, Joe Toplyn, Merrill Markoe, Chris Elliott. *Back row:* George Meyer, Randy Cohen, Kevin Curran, Tom Gammil (hat only), Andy Breckman, Gerard Mulligan, Jim Downey, Matt Wickline.